THE ESSENTIAL JEWISH BAKING COOKBOOK

the essential
JEWISH BAKING COOKBOOK

50 TRADITIONAL RECIPES FOR EVERY OCCASION

Beth A. Lee

Photography by Annie Martin

ROCKRIDGE
PRESS

Interior and Cover Designer: Stephanie Mautone
Art Producer: Sara Feinstein
Editor: Cecily McAndrews
Production Editor: Mia Moran
Production Manager: Riley Hoffman

Photography © 2021 Annie Martin. Food styling by Nadine Page. Author photo courtesy of Rosie Samuel Photography

Hardcover ISBN: 978-1-63878-611-5
Paperback ISBN: 978-1-64876-567-4
eBook ISBN: 978-1-64876-568-1
R0

To my dear Bubbe, a brilliant baker who never wrote down a recipe. May this book bring her baking back to life.

Contents

Introduction

I WISH I COULD SAY I'VE BEEN BAKING RIGHT BY MY BUBBE'S SIDE since I was five years old. The truth is, I was more of an inquisitive observer and an eager taster.

But all along, my baking bug was brewing.

Throughout my childhood, I loved watching my grandma's thick, workman-like fingers manipulate dough with ease. She spent summer after summer with us in Massachusetts kneading and rolling at the sunlit counter in the corner of the kitchen, but I waited until right before we moved to California to insist on visiting her in her tiny Brooklyn apartment to write down her challah recipe.

Scrap paper and pen in hand, my mom and I watched and wrote down Bubbe's process. A whole bag of flour (no cups or grams), "a third of a juice glass of water and as much oil and sugar." There were no actual measurements, no photos or videos of any kind. Just my hand-printed notes and my mom's in cursive on the back of an envelope.

Somehow, the scribbled recipe survived our cross-country move (and all of my moves thereafter). Miraculously, my bubbe lived to 100 and kept baking into her 90s. But her six kids didn't exactly follow suit. Four girls, two boys, no bakers. As my love for cooking blossomed, I would take out that scrappy envelope from time to time, trying to muster the courage to give challah-making a try.

While I became quite proficient at savory cooking in college, many years passed before I really dove into baking. But trust me—you don't need to wait to broaden your baking horizons. With a few simple tools, ingredients, and techniques, it's easy to get started. If you are, like me, a latecomer to baking, know that you can become a confident baker at any age.

This book will give you the recipes and the confidence you need to immerse yourself in traditional Jewish baking. It will take you back to your own precious memories of Jewish treats and help you bake some new ones. But you won't be working with barely legible notes or impossible-to-replicate measurements.

Instead, in this book you'll find 50 essential Jewish baking recipes—the ones you might remember your grandma or mom making—with all the details you need to make them a success every time.

Baking and eating are integral to Jewish culture and traditions. Think of challah for Shabbat, cookies at an Oneg, the sweets table at a wedding or bar or bat mitzvah, borekas or boyo at a family brunch. Or the cinnamon-scented coffee cake you dream about all day in temple as you eagerly await breaking the fast on Yom Kippur. Or maybe your memories include a tishpishti or sponge cake to end a festive seder meal.

But if, like me, you didn't learn to bake growing up, you can still build that tradition into your own family kitchen. Perhaps you don't identify as Jewish yourself but are married to or live with someone who does, and you want to learn more about Jewish culinary traditions. This book will be your own file of recipes both new and old so you can bake for your spouse, partner, or friends.

You'll find many classic favorites in this collection, often with carefully adapted methods and ingredients to fit our modern lifestyles. Some more advanced equipment that wasn't around in our grandmothers' kitchens—stand mixers, for one—can make bread-making easier on a busy day without sacrificing any of the joy of taking a fresh loaf of bread out of the oven.

With this book, you'll feel like my bubbe (or yours) is by your side, teaching you how the dough should feel, when the cookie is just crisp enough around the edges, how you'll know when the cake is baked. Everyone's food story is different—I hope you enjoy creating yours through the pages of this book.

CHAPTER ONE

The Jewish Bakery Intro

Every experienced home baker has their own arsenal of gadgets, equipment, and methods they can't live without in the kitchen. If you don't have experience baking, this chapter will provide the next best thing: guidance on tools and techniques to bake any recipe in the book.

My grandma's kitchen was the size of a small closet, but she baked enough to feed a large extended family along with half the neighborhood—no exaggeration. Whether you want to bake profusely or just occasionally, this chapter will give you the knowledge and confidence you need to start baking.

BUBBE'S RECIPE BOX

My bubbe's recipe box existed only in her head. She never learned to write, and even if she had, I'll never know if she would have written down any of her recipes. But this isn't the case for everyone—many people do have written recipes from their moms, aunts, grandmas, even great-grandmas. Many others have inherited old cookbooks, sometimes with hidden scraps of paper tucked inside, giving them a glimpse into old family recipes.

No two Jewish recipe boxes are alike. My personal collection is full of traditional Ashkenazi (Eastern European) Jewish recipes like rugelach, knishes, babka, and kugel. Two college friends of mine have parents who came from Greece and identify as Sephardic Jews. Their Jewish recipe box contains the likes of biscochos, borekas, and baklava. And when I visited Israel in 2017, I discovered another type of recipe box—that of Mizrahi Jews, who originate primarily from Middle Eastern or Asian countries. Mizrahi recipes include pita, lachuch, and ka'ak.

This book offers a taste from all of the above Jewish culinary traditions. If you grew up eating East Coast Ashkenazi favorites, you'll be acquainted with many of the beloved traditional recipes in these pages. But I encourage you to open up less-familiar recipe boxes as well. Borekas, an early-morning snack or lunch on the run, are found all over Israel. They may be associated with Sephardic Jews, but are eaten by many outside that demographic. Lachuch, a spongy Yemenite pita-style pancake, is found all over Israel, sometimes used like a tortilla to create what we would call a "wrap" sandwich in the United States.

I created my food blog to start documenting family recipes, and I've been fortunate to help others rediscover their own collections as well. I once gave a talk about blogging to the senior group at my temple. The youngest senior in the room raised her hand and said, "I have old Serbian recipes from my aunts who perished in the Holocaust. Should I start a blog?" From that simple question, we unearthed not only the recipes but also priceless World War II diaries from her father that she never knew existed. If you have old recipes, treasure them— they're a piece of your family history. If you don't, well, it's never too late to start a recipe box of your own.

BAKING PREP

While we may be inspired to re-create Bubbe's recipes, most of us are not cooking in Bubbe's kitchen. Our spaces are probably more expansive, our ovens larger and more feature-rich, our prep tools more efficient and abundant. But our modern amenities do not guarantee perfect results. Without a doubt, ovens with even heat, a sturdy stand mixer with a dough hook, and a cold granite or marble surface for handling dough will all help speed up steps of a recipe or improve your chance of a successful bake. But nothing replaces thorough preparation.

If you plan to bake regularly, think ahead about your workstations: where you'll roll out your dough, where you'll mix your ingredients, and where you'll store your ingredients and baking tools. In my bubbe's kitchen, there were no kitchen counters, so her workstation was her kitchen table. She had just a sink with a place to dry dishes, a stove top, and a tiny storage unit with a 1-foot-square top, if that. The kitchen table was where I watched her make challah and hamantaschen, desperately trying to decode her measurements.

Whether your kitchen is large or small, think about your ideal setup in terms of efficiency and convenience. Recipes often call for prepping your baking pans ahead of time—can you lay them out near your prep area? Do you have a place to put hot pans when they come out of the oven? (I often place them on my stove top before transferring the baked goods to a cooling rack.)

If you are short on space or have lots of flat baking trays, such as sheet pans and muffin tins, vertical storage can be very handy. In my kitchen, I've created more vertical storage by simply buying an off-the-shelf separator and placing it in a tall cabinet.

Some other questions to ask yourself before you start baking: Will you need refrigerator space to chill a tray of prepared cookie dough? Once you've finished baking, how will you store your masterpiece? Will it need refrigerator space? Freezer space? Counter space? An airtight storage container? No matter what you're baking, taking time at the beginning to think through the process from beginning to end always increases your odds of success.

Recipe 101

This might seem obvious, but it's my number one piece of advice: Read a recipe all the way through before you start baking. It's even better to read it twice. As you read through a recipe, keep the following questions in mind:

* Does it require special equipment that you don't have? If so, is there an alternative method? For example—if the recipe calls for a stand mixer, will a hand mixer work instead?

* Do you have all of the ingredients? Take out every ingredient before you start so you have them handy. Make sure you have enough of each one.

* Are there hands-off resting/chilling times involved in the bake? For example, rugelach pastries have to chill in the refrigerator before they bake. Do you have space for them to chill? Have you allotted enough time for chilling?

* Are you baking with dietary restrictions in mind (such as gluten-free, dairy-free, or kosher)? Does the recipe meet those criteria or provide alternative methods? Do you need to seek out advice on substitutions or purchase appropriate ingredients?

Measuring

Generally speaking, baking is more of an exact science than savory cooking. In savory cooking, a little extra spice or a little less protein may make no difference at all. But in baking, removing or imprecisely measuring an ingredient (or randomly changing its amount) could result in a crust that doesn't hold together, a cake that doesn't rise, a cookie that doesn't crisp, or bread that's dense as a rock.

The first time I make someone else's recipe, I follow the directions precisely so I can understand what the recipe developer was trying to achieve. Later, I might veer off the recipe's path. In baking, the more experience you have, the more you might know whether brown sugar will work in place of granulated or whether less sugar will affect the outcome. Until you're more acquainted with the basics, stay on course and take advice from those who have made the mistakes before you.

DRY INGREDIENTS

Dry-ingredient measuring cups, unlike liquid ones, must be filled to the top and evenly leveled off (using the edge of a knife, for example). Brown sugar should be compressed or "packed" into a dry measuring cup. Flour, by contrast, should not be compressed. Use a fork to aerate the flour first, then spoon it into your measuring cup and gently level it off. Alternatively, see Volume and Weight below for information on weighing your dry ingredients, a method that is quickly gaining traction in the United States. All recipes in this book offer both volume and weight measurements.

WET INGREDIENTS

Liquid measuring cups, unlike dry, do not top off at the rim. Instead, you can fill a 2-cup measuring cup to the 2-cup line without it spilling over the top. Traditional liquid measuring cups are marked with fill lines on the outside of the glass. Look for a set where you can see the fill marks on the inside of the glass. I have a 1-, 2-, and 4-cup set and absolutely love it.

VOLUME AND WEIGHT

We bought a kitchen scale a few years back, and it has become a workhorse in our kitchen, from weighing our coffee in the morning to precisely measuring ingredients for my bread baking. There's no need for individual measuring cups, glasses, and spoons. You can often use a single bowl: Just add the ingredient, zero it out (the "tare" button) and add the next. It gives more accurate measurements, and it's so easy. It may not be what you are used to, but once you try it, you'll really appreciate its simplicity.

Temps

Temperature is very important in baking as well, specifically as it relates to oven, ambient, and ingredient temperature.

OVEN TEMPERATURE

Many recipes give you a range of bake times because no two ovens are the same. Always check your baked goods at the earliest time indicated. Recipes in this book are tested on the regular setting, not convection. If you're using dark pans or glass pans, remember that your baked goods will cook more quickly.

AMBIENT TEMPERATURE

The temperature of the air in the kitchen is especially important when baking bread. The amount of rising time noted in a recipe is always an estimate, so pay more attention to how the dough looks. Dough will rise slower in colder air, and you can use that to your advantage—if you need to slow the rise down, put your dough in the refrigerator. Need to speed it up? Find a warmer spot. See The Baker's Dozen techniques (page 11) for more tips on how to know when your bread is done proofing.

INGREDIENT TEMPERATURE

When you read a recipe, look for these details in the ingredient list. For example, when creaming butter with sugar, butter must be at room temperature. By contrast, for a piecrust, butter must be cold. "Room temperature" butter should be between 65°F and 70°F.

THE BAKING KITCHEN

Remember: My grandma had few of the modern tools we have at our fingertips, yet she was still a profuse and proficient baker. As such, I'm a stickler for not buying single-use kitchen tools—so many pieces of kitchen equipment are used for both baking and savory cooking. For example, I use half-sheet pans to bake cookies and then pull another out to roast vegetables for dinner. An instant-read thermometer is great for checking the temperature of meat but just as handy for determining if the inside of your bread is cooked.

This section covers my recommendations for equipping your kitchen to bake the recipes in this book. I promise to stick to the versatile essentials—this list will not be extravagant.

Tools and Equipment

This book focuses on Jewish recipes, but any equipment you buy will be useful in your baking for years to come. I've divided my recommended equipment into a must-have list and a nice-to-have list.

MUST-HAVES

Baking pans—I recommend a 9½-inch Bundt pan, a 9-by-5-inch or 8½-by-4½-inch loaf pan, a 9-by-13-inch rectangular pan, and an 8-inch or 9-inch round springform pan.

Cooling racks—Essential for almost anything you bake.

Dry measuring cups and spoons—Either stainless steel or plastic will work.

Electric hand mixer—Handy for batters, whipped cream, and more.

Half-sheet pans (2)—Rimmed 18-by-13-inch baking sheets. They fit silicone mats and precut parchment paper perfectly.

Liquid measuring cups—Either glass or plastic—I prefer ones where you can read the measurement markings on the inside.

Mixing bowls—Various sizes in glass, ceramic, or non-slip plastic all work great.

Mixing spoons—One wooden spoon for mixing and one rubber spatula for getting all of the batter out of the bowl.

Parchment paper—Heatproof paper that provides a perfect surface for baking. It eliminates the need to grease pans directly.

Rolling pin—Either a wooden dowel-style pin or a marble one with handles.

Small and large whisk—It's helpful to have several for mixing dry ingredients and whipping wet ones without having to wash between uses.

NICE-TO-HAVES

Baking stone—A rectangular or square ceramic or stone surface preheated in the oven and used for many types of bread-baking.

Bench/dough scraper—A plastic scraper for moving dough from bowl to counter, and a sturdy metal scraper for portioning dough.

Digital kitchen scale—Once you try measuring ingredients with one, you'll be hooked, I promise.

Pastry brush—A heatproof silicone one is my favorite.

Sifter—Sometimes, a whisk won't suffice, and you need real sifted flour. In a sponge or angel food cake, for example, any lumps in the flour might weigh the cake down—consistent texture is key.

Stand mixer—Helpful for batters, whipped cream, and doughs. If you bake a lot of bread, cakes, and cookies, this becomes a must-have.

Ingredients

All-purpose flour and bread flour—If you only buy one type of flour, choose the more versatile all-purpose flour. See Flours (page 9) for more information.

Baking powder and baking soda—Both are leavening agents, but they act differently in baked goods, so do not substitute one for the other. I recommend aluminum-free baking powder.

Brown sugar—When I call for "brown sugar" in a recipe, either light or dark brown sugar is fine. Brown sugar should always be packed into a measuring cup.

Cinnamon—Several recipes in this book call for cinnamon. I recommend both ground cinnamon and cinnamon sticks, which are useful for flavoring syrups.

Cocoa powder—Keep a container of unsweetened cocoa powder on hand for some staple recipes.

Eggs—Large eggs are a must-have in your kitchen. All the recipes here were developed using large eggs.

Granulated sugar—In this book, all recipes use granulated sugar, unless otherwise noted.

Instant or active dry yeast—Instant and active dry yeast are virtually interchangeable—see Yeasts (page 9) for more information.

Kosher salt—Not all salts are the same. I developed the recipes in this book using Diamond Crystal brand kosher salt. If using table salt, use half as much salt as specified. If using Morton kosher salt, use 25 percent less than specified.

Semisweet or bittersweet chocolate chips—Helpful for when you don't have time to chop your own chocolate. When making Apricot Chocolate Rugelach (see page 64), I opt specifically for miniature chocolate chips.

Unsalted butter—All recipes in this book use unsalted butter, not European-style or salted butter, unless otherwise noted.

Vanilla extract—It's important to purchase real vanilla extract and not imitation extract. The flavor is different.

Vegetable and olive oil—Canola or any other neutral-flavored oil will work as well.

FLOURS

The recipes in this book primarily use all-purpose flour and bread flour. The difference between the two is that bread flour has a higher protein content, resulting in stronger gluten structure. However, all-purpose flour will work just as well as bread flour. Don't fret if you are making bread and only have all-purpose flour. It's called *all-purpose* for a reason.

The other flours used in this book are rye flour, whole wheat flour, and almond flour. For Deli-Style No-Knead Rye Bread and Marbled Rye Sandwich Bread (see pages 18 and 20), any rye flour marked as "rye," "medium rye," or "dark rye" will work. The darker the rye flour, the more true rye flavor your loaf will have. Pumpernickel flour is much coarser and I don't recommend it for the recipes in this book. Because rye flour has very little gluten in it, I've used it in combination with all-purpose or bread flour to get an airier loaf.

For Hearty Whole Wheat Challah (page 24), I mixed whole wheat flour with all-purpose flour. Whole wheat flour requires more moisture than regular flour, so use as directed in any given recipe.

For Chocolate-Dipped Almond Coconut Macaroons (page 80) and Light-as-Air Tishpishti (page 100), I use almond flour. It is easily sourced at grocery stores and is handy for making recipes Passover-friendly and gluten-free. Note that almond flour won't give you the solid structure of wheat flour, so it's best used as a substitution in more-delicate recipes, like cakes and cookies.

YEASTS

The recipes in this book use active dry yeast or instant yeast. The two are interchangeable, but they require different techniques. Active dry yeast traditionally requires proofing—dissolving it in liquid to confirm that it is alive (see Techniques, page 11). With that said, active dry yeasts available today have smaller granules and will also usually work if added directly to dry ingredients (without proofing). Just make sure the packet isn't expired, and if you're worried, proof it first to be safe. Instant yeast never requires proofing—you can add it directly to the dry ingredients without proofing first.

Active dry yeast is usually sold in packets of three, each containing 2¼ teaspoons (or .25 ounces) of yeast, or in a small 4-ounce jar. I always keep a few packets of active dry yeast in my baking drawer as well. For instant yeast, I recommend buying Saf-Instant Red brand yeast in a 1-pound bag. It's economical and lasts for a long time stored in an airtight container in the freezer.

Kosher Baking

If you keep a kosher kitchen, there are three key elements related to baking. First is the tools you use. Most kitchens have separate meat, dairy, and pareve tools. Pareve tools are washed in a way that keeps them free of dairy and meat. Kitchens often have separate ovens in order to cook dairy items separately from meat items.

Second is the use of certified kosher ingredients. A careful look at labels will tell you whether a product is pareve (free of dairy and meat products) and/or prepared according to kosher laws.

Third is what you plan to serve alongside any given baked good. If you make a babka with lots of butter in the recipe and plan to serve it at a dairy meal, no problem. But if you plan to serve it after a meat meal, you'll need to make substitutions.

Generally, margarine works as a one-to-one butter substitute. Not all margarines are kosher and not all are dairy-free, so look for brands that are specifically marked as pareve. If margarine is marked OU-D, it is kosher but not dairy-free.

For milk substitutes, check the label for kosher markings. Whether you choose almond, soy, coconut, oat, or any other milk alternative is a matter of preference. Not all of these recipes have been tested with milk substitutes, but if they have been, it will be noted.

You'll notice that many of the recipes in the book are "accidentally" dairy-free. Look to chapter 2 for dairy-free bread options, including Bubbe's Challah (page 22). Most Passover dessert recipes will be dairy-free, such as Citrus Sponge Cake (page 102), Light-as-Air Tishpishti (page 100), and, of course, my Flourless Chocolate Cake with Jam-Liqueur Sauce (page 96). Many cookie recipes also qualify, including Orange–Olive Oil Hamantaschen (page 58).

Techniques

In 2013, my family and I took a pizza-making class in Sorrento, Italy, from a lovely local woman. Once our pizza dough was mixed, she taught us the technique for forming the dough balls and walked away. Hesitant but determined, we formed each one as she showed us, placing it in the proofing drawer with pride. Then she came over to check, said something in Italian, and re-formed each one, in a matter of seconds, to a perfect smooth sphere. Apparently, our technique needed work.

Luckily, I'm not teaching you how to make pizza. But I *can* share a few basic baking techniques you'll use over and over. When you buy bagels or other bakery goods, you'll often get a baker's dozen—13 for the price of 12. It seems only appropriate, then, to give you 13 terms and techniques to help you navigate the recipes in the book. If a recipe uses a technique not covered here, it will be clearly explained in the recipe instructions (like the recipe for Lachuch, a Holey Yemenite Pancake, page 30).

THE BAKER'S DOZEN

1. **Creaming** (technique)—Combining sugar and fat, usually butter. This can be done by hand, but it's easiest with a hand mixer or in a stand mixer with a paddle attachment.

2. **Folding in** (technique)—Using a rubber spatula to gently mix batter as you turn the bowl.

3. **Greasing the pan** (technique)—Using nonstick cooking spray or butter with a dusting of flour, or parchment paper, to prevent baked goods from sticking to pans.

4. **Measuring flour by volume** (technique)—Using a fork or whisk to aerate the flour first, then spooning it into the measuring cup and gently leveling it off.

5. **Proofing bread dough** (term)—This refers to the resting time when dough is rising. Of course, it is the active, living yeast that makes the dough rise.

6. **Proofing yeast** (technique)—The process of making sure active dry yeast is alive. Mix the yeast into warm water (between 105°F and 115°F) with a pinch of sugar to ensure it blooms.

7. **Rolling out dough** (technique)—In general, cold surfaces are best to roll out dough. Use flour as needed to prevent sticking, and if the dough warms up too much, return it to the refrigerator to chill briefly.

8. **Room temperature** (term)—Often called for with butter or eggs. "Room temperature" refers to a range roughly between 65°F and 70°F.

9. **Separating eggs** (technique)—Easing the whites away from the yolks using each side of a cracked egg.

10. **Testing for doneness** (technique)—Often accomplished with a toothpick or cake tester inserted in a baked good. Also look for specific visual cues noted in each recipe.

11. **Testing if bread dough is done proofing** (technique)—Poke your floured finger into the dough. If it doesn't spring back at all, the dough is over-proofed. If it springs back quickly and completely, it's not ready. When it springs back slowly, it's time to bake.

12. **Toasting nuts** (technique)—Toasting nuts prior to baking adds flavor and crunch. Bake for 5 to 10 minutes at 350°F.

13. **Whipping** (technique)—A useful technique to incorporate air into a batter or liquid. Use a large whisk and some elbow grease, or an electric hand mixer or stand mixer with a whisk attachment.

KNEADING AND SHAPING

All yeasted bread recipes require kneading, shaping, and/or braiding of the dough. Deli-Style No-Knead Rye Bread (page 18) is technically a no-knead recipe, but you'll still apply a brief kneading technique to get a feel for it and pull it together. You'll then shape it into a round for its last rise. For Bubbe's Challah (page 22) and Hearty Whole Wheat Challah (page 24), you will knead, shape, and then braid the dough. Each recipe explains how to work the dough specific to that baked good, but here's a general overview to familiarize you with all three techniques.

Braiding—Challah is typically braided, though sometimes, a single strand can be formed into a turban-like round to make smaller rolls or a simple round challah. I suggest starting with a simple three-strand braid for challah. There are many more techniques to learn as you get used to the process.

Kneading—Kneading builds up the gluten structure of your bread. Bubbe did this by hand, and many bakers still prefer hand-kneading, even if they have a stand mixer with a dough hook. Kneading by hand forces you to acquaint yourself with the dough, watching it transform from a shaggy blob to a smooth, elastic ball. Kneading is simple: Place your dough on a floured kitchen counter or on a large marble or wooden board. Pull one side of the dough up, over, and into the center and use the heel of your hand to push it down and out. Repeat, turning the dough 90 degrees after each knead. You'll see and feel the dough change as you repeat and repeat.

Shaping—All yeasted breads, including challah, babka, and rye bread, require some form of shaping, usually prior to the second rise and sometimes just before baking. My best advice: Don't fear the dough. Use your hands, the work surface, and the tension in the dough to coax the dough into the desired shape. Sometimes, the dough may be too springy and unwilling to stay in place when stretching or rolling it out. If this happens, just let it rest for a few minutes, and then it will cooperate.

Dietary Substitutions

While this book is not strictly kosher, vegan, gluten-free, dairy-free, or nut allergy–sensitive, I'm well aware of the importance of dietary restrictions. Our whole family is lactose-intolerant, and we have a friend with a life-threatening peanut allergy. For as long as we've hosted Rosh Hashanah, we've asked guests to bring nut-free dishes so everyone can safely enjoy all the food.

Whenever possible, I include substitutions that may help accommodate dietary needs. While some kosher recipes include dairy, many can be made dairy-free. For example, Light-as-Air Tishpishti (page 100) lends itself to a gluten- and dairy-free approach. Using olive oil instead of butter helps meet vegan and kosher dietary requirements.

ABOUT THE RECIPES

To help you dig in and find your favorite recipes, here's how this book is organized: Chapter 2 has all the breads, from challahs to babka to flatbreads to deli-style rye. Chapter 3 is full of pastry favorites—anything rolled or stuffed, both savory and sweet. Think rugelach, borekas, and knishes. Chapter 4 is all about the sweets table, with cakes and cookies of all kinds. Chapter 5 tops it off with more treats and toppings, like soufganiyot, challah bread pudding, and fruit compote. Each recipe is labeled according to the dietary requirements it meets (gluten-free, dairy-free, vegan, nut-free, pareve). Always check package labels to confirm that the products you're using conform to dietary restrictions. Many recipes also include tips to help you along, described as follows.

Substitution tips provide suggestions for how to swap out ingredients for flavor purposes or dietary or kosher requirements.

Make-ahead tips explain how a recipe (or individual steps) can be prepared in advance.

Storage tips explain how to correctly store leftovers and for how long.

Ingredient tips provide additional information on selecting, buying, or using an ingredient.

Variation tips offer a way to enhance or change a recipe using an optional ingredient.

Kosher tips give instructions on how to adapt a recipe to meet kosher dietary requirements.

CHAPTER TWO

Challah, Babka, and Breads

‹ Sweet Challah Rolls with Apple Currant Filling

Deli-Style No-Knead Rye Bread

PREP TIME: 20 minutes • **INACTIVE TIME:** 2 hours 30 minutes to 18 hours 30 minutes •
COOK TIME: 35 minutes

My rye bread memories include spicy brown deli mustard, a sour pickle, and hot pastrami. The bread is full of caraway seeds, with a crunchy crust and chewy interior. All too often, baking deli-style rye at home is a two-day process, requiring a mature starter and a lot of patience. This flavorful loaf can be made in less than half a day, and the majority of that time is hands-off. This rye is a great leftover bread: On day two, a quick toast will bring that crunchy, chewy essence right back. ✳ MAKES 1 LOAF

3 cups (411 grams) bread
flour (all-purpose flour
also works)

1 cup (102 grams) rye flour

2¼ teaspoons
(7 grams/1 packet)
active dry yeast or
instant yeast

2 teaspoons granulated
sugar

1 tablespoon caraway
seeds for dough, plus
1 teaspoon for sprinkling
(optional)

1¾ cups (412 grams) warm
water (105°F to 115°F)

2 teaspoons kosher salt

1 teaspoon cornmeal
(optional)

1. **Mix:** In a large bowl, whisk together the bread flour, rye flour, yeast, sugar, and 1 tablespoon of caraway seeds. Add the warm water and salt and mix with a wooden spoon until all the flour is incorporated.

2. **First rise:** Cover the dough loosely with plastic wrap or a kitchen towel and let rise for at least 2 hours. You can let it sit even longer at room temperature, or place it in the refrigerator to rise overnight. If you refrigerate, bring the dough back to room temperature before proceeding.

3. **Stretch and fold:** Prepare a sheet of parchment paper and sprinkle with cornmeal (if using). Using a plastic dough scraper or rubber spatula, turn the dough onto a floured surface. Sprinkle some flour on top of the dough and your hands. Stretch the dough out from each side and fold it onto itself. Repeat 8 times. If the dough is too sticky to handle, add a bit more flour.

4. **Shape:** With the dough still on the lightly floured work surface, cup your hands around the dough to shape it into a ball using 4 quarter turns. The ball

will tighten, hold its shape, and be about 5 inches in diameter. Use your hands and the dough scraper, if necessary, to move the dough to the parchment.

5. **Second rise:** Cover loosely and let it rest for about 30 minutes.

6. **Preheat:** Preheat the oven to 450°F with a baking stone on the center shelf. If you don't have a baking stone, preheat the oven without anything in it (you'll use a baking sheet instead).

7. **Prep the dough for baking:** After 30 minutes, poke the dough—if it springs back slowly, it's ready to go in the oven. If not, let it proof longer, up to an hour. Brush some water on the outside, sprinkle with 1 teaspoon of caraway seeds (if using), and use a serrated knife to make 3 diagonal slashes in the top of the loaf (scoring).

8. **Bake:** Place the dough on the prepared parchment paper and then directly onto the baking stone (or onto a baking sheet). Bake for 30 to 35 minutes. At 20 minutes, check the top. If it is getting too dark, cover it loosely with foil. Check again at 30 minutes. The bread should have an internal temperature of 195° to 205°F and sound hollow when tapped. If the loaf is ready, transfer it to a wire cooling rack. If it hasn't reached its ideal temperature, continue baking in 5-minute increments. When done, allow the bread to cool thoroughly, up to 2 hours, before cutting.

Marbled Rye Sandwich Bread

PREP TIME: 30 minutes • **INACTIVE TIME:** 3 hours • **COOK TIME:** 45 minutes

Once you make Deli-Style No-Knead Rye Bread (page 18), this showstopper is your next must-do. You make two doughs, basically identical, adding cocoa powder to one to achieve the darker pumpernickel color. Roll each one out, stack them, and roll them up together. Once baked, the result is a perfect sandwich loaf (or a great piece of buttered toast) that looks just as good as it tastes. ✷ MAKES 1 LOAF

For the light rye dough

1¼ cups (171 grams)
   bread flour, plus more
   for shaping

¾ cup (76 grams) rye flour

1 teaspoon (3 grams)
   instant or active
   dry yeast

1 teaspoon kosher salt

1½ teaspoons cara-
   way seeds, plus more
   for topping

¾ cup (178 grams,
   plus 2 tablespoons)
   warm water (105°F to
   115°F), divided

1 tablespoon molasses

1. **Mix:** In a medium bowl, whisk together the dry ingredients for the light rye dough: bread flour, rye flour, yeast, salt, and caraway seeds. Add ¾ cup of warm water and molasses and mix well, using a wooden spoon or rubber spatula, until all the flour is incorporated. In a separate medium bowl, repeat this process for the dark rye dough, adding the cocoa powder to the dry ingredients.

2. **First rise:** Cover both bowls with plastic wrap or kitchen towels. Let rise for 1 to 2 hours, or until the dough is doubled in volume.

3. **First shape:** Use a dough scraper to transfer the light rye dough to a lightly floured surface. Form it into a rough rectangle; then roll it out to about a 9-by-12-inch rectangle. Repeat with the dark rye dough.

4. **Layer:** Stack the dark rye dough directly on top of the light rye dough—use a plastic dough scraper to help you with this if necessary.

5. **Prep:** Grease a 9- by-5-inch or 8½-by-4½-inch loaf pan with nonstick cooking spray.

For the dark rye dough

1¼ cups (171 grams) bread flour

¾ cup (76 grams) rye flour

1 teaspoon (3 grams) instant or active dry yeast

1 teaspoon kosher salt

1½ teaspoons caraway seeds

2 tablespoons unsweetened cocoa powder

¾ cup (178 grams) warm water (105°F to 115°F)

1 tablespoon molasses

Nonstick cooking spray

6. **Second shape:** Starting from the narrower edge, carefully roll the stacked doughs up into a spiral. Turn the dough over and place it in the prepared loaf pan, seam-side down.

7. **Second rise:** Cover with a kitchen towel and let the loaf rise until it's almost doubled and a bit higher than the edge of the loaf pan.

8. **Preheat:** Preheat the oven to 450°F.

9. **Final Prep:** Brush the top of the loaf using the 2 tablespoons of warm water, and sprinkle with more caraway seeds. Using a serrated knife, make three ½-inch-deep diagonal slashes in the top of the loaf (scoring).

10. **Bake:** Place the loaf pan in the oven and turn the heat down to 350°F. Bake for 35 to 45 minutes, until the bread reaches an internal temperature of 190°F to 200°F and sounds hollow when you tap it. Cool in the loaf pan until you can touch the pan, then remove the loaf from the pan to a cooling rack. Cool completely before cutting into individual slices.

Bubbe's Challah

PREP TIME: 45 minutes • **INACTIVE TIME:** 2 hours • **COOK TIME:** 30 minutes

This challah is my effort to replicate my bubbe's eggy loaf, which lives on in my food memories. It's the fabled recipe my mom and I attempted to write on scrap paper one afternoon, while watching Grandma bake. She used this supple dough every Shabbat, from her days on the Lower East Side to summers at our house in Massachusetts to her final days in Brooklyn. ✶ MAKES 2 LOAVES

For the dough

7½ cups (938 grams)
    all-purpose flour, plus
    more for kneading

2 packages (14 grams)
    active dry yeast
    or 4½ teaspoons
    instant yeast

⅓ cup (62 grams)
    granulated sugar

1 tablespoon kosher salt

2 cups (470 grams) warm
    water (105°F to 115°F)

⅓ cup (74g) vegetable oil

2 large eggs

**For the egg wash
and topping**

1 large egg

1 teaspoon water

1 tablespoon sesame
    seeds (optional)

1 tablespoon poppy seeds
    (optional)

1. **Mix:** In the bowl of a stand mixer, whisk together the flour, yeast, and sugar. Make a well in the center of the flour; add the salt, water, oil, and eggs.

2. **Knead:** Using the stand mixer fitted with the dough hook attachment, begin kneading on low speed for about 1 minute to combine the ingredients. Increase the speed to medium-low and continue kneading for 3 to 4 minutes, until the dough is smooth and pulls away from the sides of the bowl. If the dough is overly sticky or not pulling away from the sides, add flour, 1 tablespoon at a time, as necessary.

3. **First rise:** Transfer the dough to a lightly floured surface and knead it by hand a few times to ensure it's not too sticky. Form it into a round and return it to the mixer bowl. Cover and let it rise for 1 hour, or until doubled in volume.

4. **First shape:** Using a dough scraper, return the dough to the work surface. Punch the dough down and divide it into 6 equal pieces. Form each piece into a cylinder, place on a separate clean (not floured) work surface, and roll from the inside out to create a 14- to 16-inch-long rope. Repeat with the remaining pieces of dough, for 6 ropes total. Keep dough pieces/ropes covered until ready to braid.

Lay 3 strands of dough parallel to one another, a few inches apart, directly on a parchment-lined baking sheet to prepare for braiding.

The 3-strand braid is simple. Connect the three strands at one end, then right strand over center, and left strand over center.

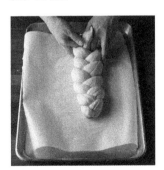

Continue this pattern until you run out of dough. Secure ends and tuck under.

5. **Second shape (braid):** Line 2 baking sheets with parchment paper. To braid a loaf, lay 3 strands parallel to one another on one of the baking sheets, a few inches apart. Pinch the 3 strands together at one end. Proceed to braid right over center, then left over center, until no dough remains. Pinch together the loose ends and tuck them underneath the loaf. Gently adjust the loaf if lopsided. Repeat with the remaining 3 strands to form a second loaf on the other baking sheet.

6. **Preheat:** Preheat the oven to 375°F. If you plan to bake both sheets at once, adjust the oven racks to the top and bottom thirds of the oven.

7. **Second rise:** Cover both loaves with a kitchen towel and let rise until nearly doubled in size, 30 minutes to 1 hour. Poke the dough with a floured finger. If the dough springs back slowly, it is ready.

8. **Egg wash:** Whisk together the egg and water for the egg wash. Use a pastry brush to completely coat each loaf with the egg wash. Sprinkle with the sesame and poppy seeds (if using).

9. **Bake:** Place the loaves in the oven and immediately lower the temperature to 350°F. Bake for 25 to 30 minutes, until the loaves' internal temperature is between 190°F and 200°F. Once baked, the loaves should sound hollow when tapped. If baking both loaves at once, rotate the oven racks halfway through baking. Remove from the oven, let rest for a couple of minutes, and transfer to a wire rack to cool to room temperature before slicing. (If you slice too early, the inside may become gummy.)

Hearty Whole Wheat Challah

PREP TIME: 30 minutes • **INACTIVE TIME:** 2 hours • **COOK TIME:** 30 minutes

This heartier version of Bubbe's challah has the added nuttiness of whole wheat flour with the same eggy flavor and soft texture as the original. It's perfect for Shabbat, for breakfast the next morning (it makes a great French toast), as an accompaniment to soup or salad, or sliced for just about any sandwich, even a good old PB&J. ✳ MAKES 1 LOAF

For the dough

2¼ teaspoons (7 grams/1 packet) active dry yeast or instant yeast

2 cups (250 grams) all-purpose flour, plus more for kneading

1½ cups (180 grams) whole wheat flour

3 tablespoons granulated sugar

1 cup (235 grams) warm water (105°F to 115°F), plus more for kneading

2 large eggs

¼ cup (56 grams) vegetable or olive oil, plus more for oiling the bowl

2 teaspoons kosher salt

For the egg wash and topping

1 large egg

1 teaspoon water

Sesame seeds or poppy seeds (optional)

1. **Mix:** In the bowl of a stand mixer, whisk the yeast, all-purpose and whole wheat flours, and sugar to combine. Add the warm water, eggs, oil, and salt.

2. **Knead:** Using the stand mixer fitted with the dough hook attachment, begin kneading on low speed to incorporate the ingredients. Gradually increase the speed to medium and knead for 3 to 5 minutes, until the dough pulls away from the sides of the bowl and a ball of dough begins to form. Stop the machine to scrape down the sides of the bowl as necessary. If the dough is too dry and won't come together, add more water a tablespoon at a time. If the dough is too sticky, add flour a tablespoon at a time. When the dough feels close to ready, transfer it to a floured work surface and knead by hand for 1 minute, until the dough feels smooth and workable.

3. **First rise:** Form the dough into a ball. Place it in an oiled bowl, cover with plastic wrap or a kitchen towel, and let it rise in a warm spot until it doubles in size, about 1½ hours.

4. **First shape:** Using a plastic scraper, transfer the dough to a floured work surface. Punch it down to deflate and divide the dough into 3 equal pieces. Using the flat side of your hand, roll each piece into a rope, starting from the middle and working

out toward the ends to create three 18- to 20-inch-long ropes. If the dough isn't cooperating, let it rest a few minutes and resume.

5. **Second shape (braid):** Line a baking sheet with parchment paper. Lay the 3 ropes parallel to one another on the baking sheet, a few inches apart. Pinch all 3 strands together at one end and braid like you would someone's hair: right over the center, then left over the center, until you reach the end. Press the loose ends together and tuck them underneath the loaf.

6. **Second rise:** Cover the loaf with a kitchen towel and let rise again for about 30 minutes, until nearly doubled in size. To check if the dough is done proofing, poke a floured finger into the dough—if the dough is ready, it should slowly spring back.

7. **Preheat:** Preheat the oven to 375°F.

8. **Egg wash:** Whisk together the egg and water and use a pastry brush to coat the loaf with the egg wash, being careful to get in all the nooks and crannies. Sprinkle the loaf with sesame seeds or poppy seeds (if using).

9. **Bake:** Bake the loaf at 375°F for 5 minutes, then lower the temperature to 350°F and continue baking for 10 minutes. Rotate the baking sheet and cook for 15 more minutes until the loaf's internal temperature is about 200°F (should sound hollow when knocked). Remove from the oven, transfer to a cooling rack, and cool to room temperature before slicing. (If you slice it too soon, the inside may become gummy.)

Sweet Challah Rolls with Apple Currant Filling

PREP TIME: 40 minutes • **INACTIVE TIME:** 30 minutes • **COOK TIME:** 30 minutes

Challah rolls filled with apples and currants are the ideal sweet baked good for Rosh Hashanah, the Jewish New Year. I originally developed this recipe for a High Holidays cooking class, but these little gems are perfect all year round. Ready faster than a traditional challah recipe, these rolls are also versatile: Leave the filling out, make one loaf instead of individual rolls, or double the recipe and freeze some for another day. ✳ MAKES 8 ROLLS

For the dough

2¼ teaspoons
(7 grams/1 packet)
active dry yeast or
instant yeast

3½ cups (438 grams)
all-purpose flour, plus
more for kneading

¼ cup (47 grams)
granulated sugar

1 cup (235 grams) warm
water (105°F to 115°F)

1 large egg

¼ cup (56 grams)
vegetable oil

1½ teaspoons kosher salt

1. **Mix:** In the bowl of a stand mixer, whisk together the yeast, flour, and sugar. Add the warm water, egg, oil, and salt.

2. **Knead:** Using the stand mixer fitted with the dough hook attachment, knead on medium-low speed for 3 to 4 minutes, making sure the dough is thoroughly combined and scraping down the sides as necessary. Once kneaded, the dough should be smooth and pulling away from the sides of the bowl. If the dough is overly sticky, add flour, 1 tablespoon at a time, as necessary.

3. **First rise:** Remove the dough from the bowl, form it into a round, and place it on a sheet of parchment paper. Use your finger to poke a 1-inch hole through the center of the dough. Cover the dough loosely with a kitchen towel and let rest for 30 minutes.

4. **Make the filling:** While the dough is resting, in a medium bowl, combine the chopped apple, lemon juice, currants, cinnamon, and sugar. Set aside.

5. **Prep:** Line a baking sheet with parchment paper.

For the filling

1 cup (118 grams) chopped
and peeled sweet
firm apple

1 teaspoon freshly
squeezed lemon juice

¼ cup (36 grams) currants
or raisins

2 teaspoons cinnamon

2 tablespoons
granulated sugar

For the egg wash

1 large egg

1 teaspoon water

Filling and shaping the rolls

6. **Fill and shape:** Divide the dough into 8 equal pieces. Flatten a piece into a roughly 6-by-4-inch rectangle and spread a heaping tablespoon of filling down the center. Close the dough up around the filling and gently roll it out with your hands to a roughly 9-inch rope. Loosely coil the rope, tuck the end under, and pinch to seal. Repeat with the remaining pieces of dough to create 8 rolls. Place on the prepared baking sheet.

7. **Second rise:** Loosely cover the challah rolls with a kitchen towel, set in a warm location, and let rise for about 30 minutes, or until the dough slowly springs back when poked with your finger.

8. **Preheat:** Preheat the oven to 375°F.

9. **Egg wash:** Whisk together the egg and water. Use a pastry brush to coat each roll with the egg wash, getting into all the nooks and crannies.

10. **Bake:** Bake the rolls for 5 minutes at 375°F, then lower the heat to 350°F and cook for about 22 minutes longer. Transfer to a wire rack and cool at least 30 minutes before serving.

Variation Tip: Use different fillings to make savory rolls or change up the sweet filling by using a different dried fruit. Alternatively, skip the stuffing and top with sesame or poppy seeds instead. To make one large loaf, braid the filled ropes as a loaf and bake for 5 to 10 additional minutes.

Roskas: A Sweet Sephardic Roll

PREP TIME: 30 minutes • **INACTIVE TIME:** 1 hour 20 minutes to 2 hours
Cook time: 20 minutes

My Sephardic friends helped unravel the mystery of these easy-to-make, fluffy rolls called roskas. Alternatively known as bolo, bucellato, rosca, and pandericas, this particular recipe is based on a variation these friends made for their mom. After testing this version, they declared the result better than their original. These are wonderful plain or with butter, cheese, olives, and/or tomatoes. They also make for a terrific little sandwich roll. ✱ MAKES 12 ROLLS

For the dough

4 cups (500 grams) all-purpose flour, plus more for kneading

2¼ teaspoons (7 grams/1 packet) active dry yeast or instant yeast

1½ teaspoons baking powder

½ teaspoon cinnamon

⅓ cup (63 grams) granulated sugar

½ cup (112 grams) vegetable oil (or any neutral oil)

1½ cups (353 grams) warm water (105°F to 115°F)

1 teaspoon kosher salt

For the egg wash and topping

1 large egg

1 teaspoon water

Sesame seeds, for sprinkling

1. **Mix:** In the bowl of a stand mixer, whisk together the flour, yeast, baking powder, cinnamon, and sugar. Add the oil, warm water, and salt.

2. **Knead:** Using the stand mixer fitted with the dough hook attachment, knead for 5 to 7 minutes, scraping down the sides as necessary. If the dough is very sticky, add flour 1 tablespoon at a time until the dough starts to pull away from the sides of the bowl.

3. **First rise:** Transfer the dough from the mixing bowl to a lightly floured work surface and knead a few times to get a feel for the dough. Form into a ball, return it to the mixing bowl, cover with a kitchen towel, and let rise until doubled in size, about 1 hour.

4. **First shape:** Line a baking sheet with parchment paper. Punch down the dough to deflate, transfer it to the work surface, and form it into a long log. Divide the log into 12 equal-size pieces. Tuck the cut ends of each piece under to form into a ball; then cup your hands around each and roll it around on a smooth surface to form a more cohesive ball.

5. **Rest:** Set each ball aside to rest on a floured counter or parchment paper for a few minutes.

6. **Second shape:** Roll each ball into a 10- to 12-inch rope. Dust each rope with flour and quickly knot it; then place the knot on the baking sheet. Repeat for all 12, spacing them about 2 inches apart on the baking sheet.

7. **Second rise:** Cover the baking sheet with a kitchen towel and let the knots rise for up to 1 hour. Check the dough every 20 minutes because rising time varies; but the dough should increase in volume by about 50 percent.

8. **Preheat:** Preheat the oven to 375°F.

9. **Egg wash:** Whisk together the egg and water. Use a pastry brush to coat each knot with the egg wash and sprinkle with sesame seeds to your taste.

10. **Bake:** Bake for 20 minutes, rotating the baking sheet halfway through. Once baked, transfer to a wire rack and let cool for a few minutes before digging in.

Variation Tip: Experiment with different toppings for these versatile rolls, such as flake salt, poppy seeds, or nigella seeds.

Lachuch, a Holey Yemenite Pancake

PREP TIME: 10 minutes • **INACTIVE TIME:** 1 hour • **COOK TIME:** 4 minutes each

The beauty of this holey pancake is its versatility. In Israel, I've eaten it as a tortilla wrapped around local cheese, za'atar, and tomatoes. In a tiny Yemenite-owned shop in Tel Aviv, I had it prepared with eggs, grated tomato, and zhug, a spicy green sauce. If you've eaten Ethiopian food, you'll recognize lachuch as a close cousin of injera, with yeasty overtones and a spongy texture. The secret to the holes on top is all in the technique. Once you master them, they're the perfect receptacle for the juices of a hearty soup or stew. ✳ MAKES 10 PANCAKES

3 cups (375 grams) all-purpose flour

2¼ teaspoons (7 grams/1 packet) active dry yeast or instant yeast

1 to 2 teaspoons fenugreek leaves (optional)

2 teaspoons kosher salt

¾ teaspoon baking soda

3 cups (706 grams) warm water (105°F to 115°F), plus up to ¼ cup more to thin the batter

Oil, for greasing pan

1. **Mix:** In a large bowl, whisk together the flour, yeast, and fenugreek (if using). Add the salt, baking soda, and 3 cups of water. Mix with a wooden spoon until all the flour is incorporated. The consistency should be like pancake batter.

2. **Rise:** Cover the bowl with a kitchen towel and set aside to rise for about an hour. You should see lots of bubbles, and the dough should look pillowy when ready to use.

3. **Prep:** Line a baking sheet with paper towels and pour some oil into a small bowl. Dip a paper towel into the oil and use it to grease the interior of a 10-inch nonstick skillet with a lid.

4. **Add water:** Just before cooking, add water to the batter, 1 tablespoon at a time (up to ¼ cup), and whisk gently until the mixture feels like a pourable batter—thick but not too viscous.

5. **Cook:** Ladle ½ cup of batter into the still-cold skillet, moving the pan around as needed to help the batter spread. Turn the heat to medium-high and cook the pancake for 3 minutes, rotating the pan 180 degrees halfway through. (Do not flip.). Lachuch cooks from the outside in, and bubbles gradually form on top. When all wet batter on top has disappeared, cover the pan for about 30 seconds to finish cooking. The underside should be golden brown, and the top will be pale and full of holes. Transfer the finished pancake to the prepared baking sheet. Repeat with the remaining batter, using the oiled paper towel to re-grease the skillet between pancakes. To cool the skillet between lachuch, run the bottom of it under cold water. Serve lachuch hot or at room temperature.

6. **Store:** Store leftover lachuch at room temperature for up to 2 days, or refrigerate for up to 5 days.

Make-ahead Tip: The batter will keep in the refrigerator overnight—just return it to room temperature before using (the batter should be bubbly).

Malawach, Yemenite Flatbread

PREP TIME: 30 minutes • **INACTIVE TIME:** 2 to 24 hours • **COOK TIME:** 4 minutes each

A Yemenite specialty, malawach is a crispy, layered flatbread that shares many similarities with Indian parathas. The nigella seeds, also known as kalonji or black seeds, add a nutty, almost onion-like flavor. The dough is strikingly beautiful when rolled out, and the first bite of the flaky bread out of the pan always puts a big smile on my face. Once you get the hang of preparing the dough rounds, you'll want to make a double batch so you always have a stash in the freezer to fry up on demand. ✳ MAKES 8 ROUND FLATBREADS

4 cups (500 grams) all-purpose flour

1 cup (235 grams) warm water (105°F to 115°F), plus more for kneading

1 tablespoon kosher salt

½ cup (1 stick/114 grams) unsalted butter, melted and cooled to room temperature

Nigella seeds (optional)

1. **Knead:** In the bowl of a stand mixer fitted with the dough hook attachment, combine the flour, water, and salt. Knead on low speed until the dough comes together and pulls away from the sides of the bowl, 3 to 5 minutes. If the dough is too dry, add water, a tablespoon at a time, as needed. Note that this is a fairly sturdy dough that becomes more supple after it rests.

2. **Rest:** Cover the dough with plastic wrap and let it rest for 30 minutes.

3. **Prep:** Clear a clean work surface. Place the melted butter, a pastry brush, a rolling pin, and a platter that can fit in the refrigerator within reach.

4. **First shape:** Divide the dough into 8 equal pieces. Spread some of the melted butter on the work surface, covering a 12-by-12-inch area. Use your palm to flatten 1 piece of dough, place it on the buttered surface, and roll it out into a 12-by-10-inch rectangle, rolling it as thinly as possible without tearing. Brush the melted butter over the dough and sprinkle on nigella seeds (if using).

5. **Second shape:** Roll the thin rectangle of dough up into a log, starting from the long edge—fold the dough over about ½ inch at first, then continue rolling until no dough is left. Roll the log into a coil, like a snail, and pinch the ends to seal. Place it on the prepared platter. Repeat steps 4 and 5 with the remaining dough, re-buttering the work surface as needed.

6. **Chill:** Cover with plastic wrap and refrigerate the coils for at least 1 hour or overnight.

7. **Final shape:** About 1 hour before you are ready to cook them, take the coils out of the refrigerator and roll each into an 8-inch round. Layer on a plate with wax paper or parchment paper in between each.

8. **Freeze:** Place the rounds in the freezer for at least 30 minutes, or until frozen solid. (Or, wrap them tightly and store frozen until ready to panfry.)

9. **Panfry:** Heat a cast-iron pan or medium skillet over medium to medium-high heat. Place a frozen dough round directly in the pan and cook for about 2 minutes per side. It should be brown in spots, appear to be flaky and a bit puffy. Repeat with the remaining rounds. (Malawach should cook with no additional butter, but if they're sticking, you can butter the pan lightly.)

Maya's Pillowy Pita

PREP TIME: 40 minutes • **INACTIVE TIME:** 1 hour 30 minutes • **COOK TIME:** 12 minutes total if cooking 2 at a time

When your niece-by-choice becomes the head baker at one of the best bread shops in Northern California and then offers you their pita recipe, you accept. The signature element of a pita is the pocket that's created when it puffs up while baking, perfect for stuffing with falafel, eggplant, hummus, or any protein, spread, or vegetable you choose. One of my favorite ways to serve pita is slathered with olive oil, za'atar, and sliced tomatoes. Reheat, slice like a pizza, and thank me later. ✳ MAKES 12 PITAS

4 cups bread flour
(548 grams) (all-purpose
flour will also work)
2 packets active dry
yeast (14 grams)
or 4½ teaspoons
instant yeast
2 teaspoons
granulated sugar
1 tablespoon plus
1 teaspoon kosher salt
1⅓ cups (314 grams) warm
water (105°F to 115°F),
plus more for kneading
2 tablespoons olive oil or
other neutral oil, plus
more for oiling the bowl

1. **Mix:** In the bowl of a stand mixer, whisk together the flour, yeast, and sugar. Add the salt, 1⅓ cups of warm water, and the oil.

2. **Knead:** Using the stand mixer fitted with the dough hook attachment, knead on low speed for at least 5 minutes, until the dough pulls away from the sides of the bowl and is smooth and moist but not sticky. If the dough is not coming together, add 1 to 2 tablespoons of water, 1 tablespoon at a time.

3. **First rise:** Place the dough in a lightly oiled bowl, cover with a kitchen towel, and let rise until doubled in volume, about 1 hour.

4. **Preheat and Prep:** Preheat the oven to 500°F with a baking stone on the center rack. Line 2 baking sheets with parchment paper.

5. **First shape:** Place the dough on a lightly floured surface, punch it down, divide the dough into 12 equal pieces, and keep covered with a kitchen towel. Form each piece into a ball by folding the uneven edges under. Cup your hand loosely around the dough ball and roll it over a smooth,

unfloured work surface to form it into a smooth sphere. Place on the prepared baking sheet. Repeat with remaining pieces and cover loosely. If you are not ready to bake the pitas, you can keep the balls loosely but completely covered and place them in the refrigerator. Bring to room temperature before proceeding to the next step.

6. **Roll out and rest:** With a rolling pin, roll each ball on a clean surface into a flat circle about ¼ inch thick and 4 to 5 inches in diameter. If needed, gently flour the rolling pin. Place each round onto the prepared baking sheets and let rest, covered with a kitchen towel, for about 30 minutes.

7. **Bake:** Place 2 pitas directly on the well-heated stone and bake for 30 to 45 seconds on the first side, flip over and cook for 30 seconds on the second side, then flip again and watch them puff. If they don't puff, don't despair. Pitas are finicky and occasionally don't puff, but most of the time they will. The key is to flip quickly before they cook through and to be sure the baking stone is good and hot. You'll get the feel of the stone and oven after cooking the first batch, and you can adjust the bake time up or down. Place cooked pitas on a towel after baking and wrap to conserve the moisture and keep them soft. Serve warm or room temperature. Store leftovers at room temperature in an airtight container for up to 2 days.

Ready-for-Lox Homemade Bagels

PREP TIME: 45 minutes • **INACTIVE TIME:** 6 to 18 hours • **COOK TIME:** 1 hour

I used to think bagels could only be a store-bought treat. My family got them exclusively from a New York–style water bagel bakery, and they were always crispy, chewy, and just the right size. It turns out that with a little bit of prep work, you can eat water bagels fresh out of the oven—*your oven*—any time you want. Bagel dough is a stiff dough for kneading, but that makes it easy to manipulate into a perfect bagel shape. Bread flour is definitely preferable to all-purpose flour here, because it gives us the signature chewy texture we expect. ✴ MAKES 12 BAGELS

For the dough

6 cups (822 grams) bread flour

2¼ teaspoons (7 grams/1 packet) active dry yeast or instant yeast

2 cups (470 grams) warm water (105°F to 115°F)

1 tablespoon barley malt syrup

1 tablespoon kosher salt

For the boiling liquid

2 to 4 tablespoons barley malt syrup

1 teaspoon baking soda

2 teaspoons kosher salt

For the topping

¼ to ½ cup sesame, poppy, or nigella seeds, or everything bagel seasoning (optional)

1. **Mix:** In the bowl of a stand mixer, whisk the bread flour and yeast together. Add the water, barley malt syrup, and salt.

2. **Knead:** Using the stand mixer fitted with the dough hook attachment, knead on low speed for 7 minutes, until the mixture combines and forms a dough ball. You may need to stop the machine once or twice to scrape down the sides of the bowl. This makes a very stiff dough, so if the stand mixer is having a hard time, transfer the dough to a floured surface and knead by hand. The dough will be very smooth and stiff once fully kneaded.

3. **First rise:** Form the dough into a round by cupping your hands around it and shaping it into a ball using 4 quarter turns. Place in a bowl, cover it with plastic wrap or a kitchen towel, and let it rise until doubled in size, 1½ to 2 hours.

4. **First shape:** Line 2 baking sheets with parchment paper. Punch the dough down to deflate it and transfer it to a clean work surface (no flour necessary). Separate the dough into 12 equal pieces. Turn each piece into a round ball by gathering the uneven edges underneath, then cupping

your hand around the dough ball and gliding it around the work surface to even out the rough edges. Repeat with each dough ball, and keep the finished dough balls covered.

5. **Second shape:** Working 1 piece at a time, poke a hole in the dough ball, and gently but firmly stretch it into a bagel shape. The hole should be about 2 inches in diameter, and the whole bagel about 4 inches across. Once baked, the hole will shrink. When all bagels are formed, cover the baking sheets tightly with plastic wrap and place in the refrigerator overnight.

6. **Preheat:** The next day, preheat the oven to 425°F. (Once the bagels are boiled and drained, they will need to go directly into the oven.)

7. **Prepare to boil:** Fill a large, widemouthed pot with water and bring to a rolling boil over high heat. Place a wire rack on top of a baking sheet to drain the bagels. If you plan to use toppings, place them on plates wide enough to dip the bagels.

8. **Float test:** Take the formed bagels out of the refrigerator and do a "float test" by placing 1 bagel in a bowl filled with room-temperature water (65°F to 70°F). If it floats, you're ready to boil. If it doesn't, return the bagel to the baking sheet and continue proofing for 15 minutes—then check again.

CONTINUED ▶

9. **Boil:** Once the water is boiling, add the barley malt syrup, baking soda, and salt. The water should look somewhat like black tea. If you're using a large pot, you may need a little extra malt syrup. Add the first 6 bagels and boil for 1 minute each, flipping halfway. If a bagel starts to bubble, use a large-slotted spoon to remove it from the pot. Place boiled bagels on the wire rack to drain immediately.

10. **Add the topping:** Top each bagel by dipping one side in the plates with the topping (if using). Repeat the boiling and topping process with the remaining bagels.

11. **Bake:** Place the boiled, topped bagels on one of the baking sheets, at least an inch apart. Bake for 18 to 20 minutes, checking at 18. They should be brown and have tiny blister marks on them. Place on a wire rack to cool for a few minutes, then serve warm (preferably with lox and cream cheese). Repeat steps 9 and 10 with the remaining 6 bagels while the first 6 are baking, then repeat step 11 with the remaining 6 bagels.

PLetzel, Not PRetzel!

PREP TIME: 25 minutes • **INACTIVE TIME:** 12 to 14 hours • **COOK TIME:** 50 minutes

If focaccia and a bialy had a baby, it would be a pletzel. Pletzels likely originated in Bialystock, Poland, like their bialy relatives. Sometimes called onion boards, they were once sold widely in Jewish bakeries, but are now rarely seen. This is my effort to bring them back. ✳ MAKES 1 LARGE SLAB

For the dough

3 cups (375 grams) all-purpose flour

2¼ teaspoons (7 grams/1 packet) active dry yeast or instant yeast

2 teaspoons kosher salt, plus more for topping

2 tablespoons olive oil, plus more to coat the dough

1¼ cups (294 grams) warm water (105°F to 115°F)

For the topping

2 tablespoons olive oil

1 large yellow onion (about ¾ pound), finely chopped

½ teaspoon kosher salt

2 teaspoons poppy seeds

Flake or kosher salt to taste (optional)

1. **Mix:** In a large bowl, whisk together the flour and yeast. Add the salt, olive oil, and warm water and mix with a wooden spoon or rubber spatula until all the flour is incorporated. Rub a teaspoon or less of olive oil over the dough, cover with plastic wrap or a kitchen towel, and set in the refrigerator overnight. It will get bubbly and double in size.

2. **Make the topping:** In a medium sauté pan, heat the olive oil and onion over medium-low heat. Sauté the onion, stirring frequently, for 15 to 20 minutes, or until translucent and just starting to brown. When nearly done, stir in the salt.

3. **Preheat:** Preheat the oven to 425°F.

4. **Stretch the dough:** Line a baking sheet with parchment, and brush with about 2 teaspoons of olive oil. Gently scrape the dough onto the baking sheet. Let it rest for 5 minutes. Using your fingers in a dimple motion, stretch the dough into a 13-by-10-inch rectangle. If the dough shrinks back, cover loosely and let it rest for 20 to 30 minutes. Stretch again.

5. **Add the toppings:** Spread the sautéed onion all over the dough, leaving a 1-inch border. Sprinkle with the poppy seeds and a touch of salt (if using).

6. **Bake:** Bake for 30 minutes, rotating the pan halfway. Transfer to a wire rack. Cool slightly and cut into squares to eat warm.

Jerusalem Bagel Pretzel

PREP TIME: 30 minutes • **INACTIVE TIME:** 1 hour 30 minutes to 2 hours • **COOK TIME:** 40 minutes

A popular street food in Jerusalem, these oblong sesame bread beauties are closer in texture to a soft pretzel than a bagel. The baked treats are known as ka'ak Al-Quds in Arabic (ka'ak means "cake" and Al-Quds translates to "Jerusalem"). My tour guide in Israel described them perfectly: They feel barely baked, airy light, and are countered by the thin, crisp sesame skin. Of course, they're not complete without some salty, herby za'atar on the side for dipping. ✳ MAKES 6 BAGELS

For the dough

2¼ teaspoons
(7 grams/1 packet)
active dry yeast or
instant yeast

4 cups (500 grams)
all-purpose flour

1 teaspoon baking powder

2 tablespoons instant dry
milk powder

1 tablespoon plus
1 teaspoon kosher salt

1¼ cups (294 grams) warm
water (105°F to 115°F)

2 tablespoons olive oil,
plus more for greasing

3 tablespoons honey

For the egg wash
and topping

1 large egg

1 teaspoon water

½ cup sesame seeds

1 teaspoon kosher or flake
salt (optional)

1. **Mix:** In the bowl of a stand mixer, whisk together the yeast, flour, baking powder, and milk powder. Add the salt, warm water, oil, and honey.

2. **Knead:** Using the stand mixer fitted with the dough hook attachment, knead on low speed for 4 to 5 minutes, until the dough comes together. If necessary, stop the machine briefly to scrape down the sides. Once kneaded, the dough should be smooth, elastic, and not sticky.

3. **First rise:** Remove the dough from the bowl and form it into a ball. Return it to a lightly oiled mixing bowl, cover it with plastic wrap or a kitchen towel, and set it aside to rise until doubled in size, about an hour.

4. **First shape:** Punch down the dough to deflate and transfer it to a clean work surface. Divide the dough into 6 equal pieces. Cover the dough pieces you're not using with a kitchen towel to prevent drying out. Form each piece into a nice round ball by folding the rough edges under to start rounding. Cup your hand loosely around the dough ball and glide it around the work surface to remove uneven spots. As you form each ball, keep the entire batch covered. Let them rest for about 10 minutes.

5. **Preheat/Prep:** Preheat the oven to 375°F. Line 2 baking sheets with parchment paper.

6. **Second shape:** After the dough balls have rested, take 1 ball at a time and poke a hole in the middle. Working gently but firmly, stretch the hole to at least 7 or 8 inches. The dough is tough, so be assertive with your stretching. Place 3 shaped bagels on each prepared baking sheet.

7. **Second rise:** Cover the bagels with a kitchen towel and let rise for 15 minutes to 1 hour until they puff up a bit (they won't double in size.)

8. **Egg wash:** While waiting for second rise, make the egg wash by whisking together the egg and water. After the second rise, use a pastry brush to brush the egg wash onto each bagel and sprinkle generously with the sesame seeds and a bit of salt (if using). You could do this to both sides of the bagel to mimic the full sesame coating you would typically see in Jerusalem.

9. **Bake:** Bake the first sheet of bagels on the middle rack for 16 to 18 minutes, until just starting to brown but not dark. Repeat with the second sheet. Eat them while they're hot if possible, or reheat briefly if eating later.

Technique Tip: Use the same spoon to measure the olive oil and the honey. Measure the olive oil first, and the honey will easily slide off the spoon.

Onion-Scented Bialys

PREP TIME: 30 minutes • **INACTIVE TIME:** 3 to 4 hours • **COOK TIME:** 45 minutes

Thought to originate in the Polish town of Bialystock, these onion-filled rolls, originally called bialystocker kuchen, have all but disappeared from Poland. Luckily, as Jews left Poland and headed to America in the late 19th and early 20th centuries, along came their beloved bialy. Sometimes compared to pizza dough but most often likened to bagels, a bialy has a charm, texture, and flavor all its own. This recipe uses the same onion topping as PLetzel, Not PRetzel! (page 39). ✶ MAKES 10 BIALYS

For the dough

1 teaspoon (3½ grams)
   active dry yeast or
   instant yeast
4 cups (548 grams)
   bread flour, plus more
   for dusting
2 teaspoons (7 grams)
   kosher salt
1½ cups (354 grams) warm
   water (105°F to 115°F)

For the topping

2 tablespoons olive oil,
   plus more for greasing
   the bowl
1 medium onion,
   finely chopped
½ teaspoon kosher salt

1. **Mix:** In the bowl of a stand mixer, whisk together the yeast and bread flour. Add the salt and warm water.

2. **Knead:** Using the stand mixer fitted with the dough hook attachment, knead the dough on low speed for 1 to 2 minutes. The dough will look a bit shaggy at first. Turn the speed up a notch or two and continue kneading for about 5 more minutes. The dough should be smooth, elastic, and not sticky.

3. **First rise:** Remove the dough from the bowl, form into a ball, and place in a bowl greased with olive oil. Rub a bit of oil on the top of the dough as well so it doesn't dry out. Cover the bowl with plastic wrap or a kitchen towel and set aside to rise for 2 hours, or until doubled in size.

4. **First shape:** Line 2 baking sheets with parchment paper. Punch the dough down to deflate and place it on a clean work surface. Divide it into 10 equal balls of dough, and keep the dough pieces covered with the kitchen towel to keep them from drying out. Turn each piece into a nice round sphere by folding in and tucking the ragged edges under to start the rounding. Then cup your hand loosely

Serving bialys

around the dough ball and glide it around the work surface to smooth out uneven areas. Place the dough ball on the prepared baking sheet. Repeat with other dough pieces.

5. **Second rise:** Lightly dust the tops of the dough balls with flour and cover loosely with plastic wrap or a kitchen towel. Set the dough aside to rise again for 2 hours, until doubled in size.

6. **Make the topping:** In a medium sauté pan, heat the olive oil and sauté the onion over medium-low heat, stirring frequently for 15 to 20 minutes, or until translucent and just starting to brown. When nearly done, add the salt and mix well.

7. **Preheat/Prep:** Preheat the oven to 475°F. Place a baking stone on the center rack.

8. **Second shape:** Take 1 ball at a time, and use your thumbs to press into it, creating a thin indented center with a raised donut-like ring around edges. Place the shaped bialy dough on the prepared baking sheet and push the indented center as flat as possible. Push the dough outward toward the raised donut-like ring, similar to how you would push the bottom of a piecrust to fit in a pie pan. The indented area in the center should be at least 3 inches across and about 1/8 inch thick. Use a fork to poke holes in the bottom of the bialy, all the way to the edges of the ring. Repeat this step to form 9 more bialys. For a classic finish, dust each formed bialy with flour. Then dollop about 1 teaspoon of the onion filling in the center. Resist overfilling.

CONTINUED ▶

9. **Bake:** If using the stone, place the parchment paper with bialys directly onto the baking stone to bake. If you don't have a baking stone, place one parchment-lined baking sheet with formed bialys onto the center rack of the oven. Bake for 10 to 12 minutes. Repeat with the second baking sheet. As the bialys cook, the donut rings will get bigger, and the indentations will shrink. If the centers puff up, don't be alarmed—they'll still taste fantastic, especially when they're hot.

Storage Tip: Bialys are best hot out of the oven or eaten the same day they are baked, but they do freeze well. Freeze extras and defrost as you want to eat them, reheating in the oven or toaster oven.

Kokosh, Beigli's and Babka's Cousin

PREP TIME: 45 minutes • **INACTIVE TIME:** 45 minutes • **COOK TIME:** 30 minutes

Kokosh is a Hungarian chocolate-filled roll frequently compared to a Polish babka. Unlike babka, the dough doesn't need to rise, so in terms of time and effort, the process from start to finish is more like making a simple cake or cookie. This decadent rolled cake is similar to another Hungarian specialty, beigli, which is a yeasted roll filled with poppy seeds or nuts. For this recipe, I took cues from the dough in my neighbor's family recipe for traditional beigli. The filling closely mimics the chocolate filling of a babka. ✳ MAKES 2 ROLLS

For the dough

2¼ teaspoons (7 grams) active dry yeast or instant yeast

3 cups (375 grams) all-purpose flour, plus more for kneading

¼ cup (47 grams) granulated sugar

1 teaspoon kosher salt

¼ cup (59 grams) warm water (105°F to 115°F)

2 large eggs

⅓ cup (83 grams) freshly squeezed orange juice

1 teaspoon grated orange zest

1¼ sticks (255 grams) unsalted butter, softened

1. **Mix:** In the bowl of a stand mixer, whisk together the yeast, flour, and granulated sugar. Add the salt, warm water, eggs, orange juice, and orange zest.

2. **Knead:** Using the stand mixer fitted with the dough hook attachment, begin kneading on low speed to combine well. Add the softened butter and continue kneading for 3 to 5 minutes, turning up the speed a notch or two. The dough should ball up and come away from the sides of the bowl. If it's really sticky, add flour 1 tablespoon at a time.

3. **First rest:** Remove the dough from the bowl and place it on a clean work surface. Bring it together into a ball, place it back in the bowl, cover with plastic wrap, and refrigerate it while you make the filling.

4. **Make the filling:** In a small saucepan, melt the butter over medium-low heat. Once the butter starts to melt, add the chocolate chips and stir constantly until the mixture becomes liquid and shiny. Turn off the heat. Add the brown sugar, cocoa powder, vanilla, salt, powdered sugar, and espresso powder (if using), and mix well.

CONTINUED ▶

For the filling

¼ cup (½ stick/57 grams) unsalted butter, room temperature

½ cup (84 grams) semisweet chocolate chips (or any chopped semisweet or dark chocolate)

⅔ cup (147 grams) brown sugar

⅓ cup (32 grams) unsweetened cocoa powder

2 teaspoons vanilla

1 teaspoon kosher salt

2 tablespoons powdered sugar

½ teaspoon espresso powder (optional)

2 tablespoons vegetable oil, for brushing on dough

1 teaspoon cinnamon, to sprinkle on filling

2 teaspoons granulated sugar, to sprinkle on filling

For the egg wash

1 large egg

1 teaspoon water

5. **Prep/Preheat:** Preheat the oven to 350°F. Line a baking sheet with parchment paper.

6. **First shape:** Remove the dough from the refrigerator and divide it into 2 equal pieces. Using your hands, roughly form the dough into a rectangle and use a rolling pin to roll it out to an 11-by-14-inch rectangle (⅛- to ¼-inch thick). Spread 1 tablespoon of oil on each piece of dough, then spread half the chocolate filling on each piece, leaving a ½-inch margin on all sides. Sprinkle ½ teaspoon of cinnamon and 1 teaspoon of granulated sugar all over the chocolate.

7. **Second shape:** Roll the dough up from the shorter edge, folding the clean edge over and then gently continuing to roll it all the way up into a log. Lay the log on the prepared baking sheet, seam-side down. Using your hands or a rolling pin, gently flatten the whole log to really compress the layers. Repeat steps 6 and 7 with the other half of the dough.

8. **Second rest:** Cover the baking sheet loosely with a kitchen towel or plastic wrap and let the rolls rest for 30 to 45 minutes. Prepare the egg wash by whisking together the egg and the water.

9. **Bake:** Poke holes in the rolls on the sides and top, pushing into the center. Brush the egg wash on each roll and bake in the oven on the center rack for 30 minutes, until nicely browned. Let cool on a wire rack for at least 30 minutes before slicing and serving.

A Hero's Chocolate Babka

PREP TIME: 45 minutes • **INACTIVE TIME:** 4 hours 30 minutes to overnight
COOK TIME: 45 minutes

There's a famous *Seinfeld* episode in which Elaine and Jerry miss out on the last chocolate babka at the bakery. As they watch their friends buy it, Elaine exclaims, "They got the last babka—they're gonna be heroes!" You'll be a hero, too, if you make this sweet, eggy bread laced with chocolate, pecans, and just a hint of citrus. Slices reveal tantalizing layers of chocolate in a babka that looks just as spectacular as it tastes. ✴ MAKES ONE 8½-BY-4½-INCH LOAF (OR ONE 9-BY-5-INCH LOAF)

For the dough

2 cups (250 grams) all-purpose flour, plus more for kneading

2¼ teaspoons (7 grams/1 packet) active dry yeast or instant yeast

¼ cup (47 grams) granulated sugar

1 teaspoon grated lemon zest or orange zest

½ teaspoon kosher salt

1 large egg plus 1 yolk

¼ cup plus 2 tablespoons (3 ounces or 92 grams) warm milk (105°F to 115°F)

5 tablespoons (71 grams) unsalted butter, cut into ½-inch cubes, room temperature

Olive oil, for greasing the bowl and pan

1. **Mix:** In the bowl of a stand mixer, whisk together the flour, yeast, sugar, and lemon zest. Add the salt, egg, egg yolk, and milk.

2. **Knead:** Using the stand mixer fitted with the dough hook attachment, knead on low speed for about 2 minutes, scraping down the sides of the bowl as necessary. When the mixture is mostly combined, add the softened butter, 2 cubes at a time, mixing after each addition until incorporated. This process should take about 5 minutes. After all the butter is added, continue to knead for 8 to 10 minutes, scraping the bowl as necessary. If the dough is overly sticky, add flour, 1 tablespoon at a time, until the dough is smooth, slightly sticky, and elastic.

3. **First rise:** Form the dough into a ball and place it into an oiled bowl. Cover with plastic wrap and let rise until doubled in size, 2 to 3 hours. (Alternatively, place it in the refrigerator to rise overnight and make fresh babka in the morning.)

CONTINUED ▶

For the filling

½ **cup (88 grams) semisweet or dark chocolate chips**

¼ **cup (½ stick/57 grams) unsalted butter**

2 **tablespoons granulated sugar**

2 **tablespoons brown sugar**

2 **tablespoons unsweetened cocoa powder**

¼ **teaspoon kosher salt**

½ **teaspoon cinnamon (optional)**

¼ **cup toasted and chopped pecans (optional)**

For the glaze

¼ **cup (47 grams) granulated sugar**

¼ **cup (59 grams) water**

4. **Make the filling:** In a small, heavy-bottom saucepan, melt the chocolate and butter together over medium-low heat. Turn the heat off and add the granulated sugar, brown sugar, cocoa powder, and salt and stir well. Set aside to cool while you form the babka. Once cooled, the filling should be spreadable like peanut butter.

5. **Prep:** Clear a clean work area. Grease an 8½-by-4½-inch loaf pan; then line it with parchment paper, allowing 1 to 2 inches of overhang on each end to create handles to pull the babka out of the pan.

6. **First shape and fill:** Form the dough into a rectangle and roll it out to at least a 15-by-10-inch rectangle on a clean work surface, with the long edge closest to you. Spread the cooled filling on the rectangle, leaving a ½-inch border around the edges. Sprinkle the filling with the cinnamon and pecans (if using).

7. **Second shape:** Starting with the long edge closest to you, roll the dough up like a log. Pinch along the seam to be sure it seals; then place the log seam-side down on the work surface. Using a serrated knife, gently cut the roll in half lengthwise (yes, that's right—lengthwise). You'll end up with 2 halves revealing the layers of dough and filling. With these cut sides facing up, pinch the halves together at one end. Lift the right half over the left half and repeat, twisting the halves around each other. Pinch the halves together at the other end. You should have formed a twist, with the filling and layers exposed. Place the twist in the prepared loaf pan, pushing it in a bit from each end so it fits.

Forming a twist

8. **Second rise:** Cover the babka with a kitchen towel or plastic wrap and let rise at room temperature for up to 1½ hours, or until it expands in volume by about 30 percent. (You can accelerate this rise by placing the dough in a warmer environment like a proofing drawer.) If the dough slowly springs back when poked, it's ready to bake.

9. **Preheat:** Preheat the oven to 350°F.

10. **Bake:** Bake the babka for 45 minutes, or until the top is brown and the internal temperature reaches at least 190°F.

11. **Make the simple syrup:** While the babka bakes, place the granulated sugar and water in a small saucepan and heat over medium-low heat until the sugar dissolves. Set aside to cool.

12. **Cool:** Remove the babka from the oven and immediately brush with the simple syrup, particularly where the dough is exposed. Remove the babka from the pan using the parchment paper "handles" and cool on a wire rack for about an hour before slicing.

CHAPTER THREE

Sweet and Savory Pastries

◀ Hermine's Hamantaschen

Shortcut Apple Strudel

PREP TIME: 20 minutes • **COOK TIME:** 30 minutes

Apple strudel is often made with phyllo dough or a homemade strudel dough stretched thin enough to be see-through. But in a pinch, a store-bought puff pastry makes a great stand-in. When puff pastry is rolled thin, it becomes flaky and phyllo-like. Use a mix of tart and sweet apples for the most complex flavor, and serve with ice cream, whipped cream, or on its own, piping hot out of the oven. ✳ SERVES 6

For the filling

3 medium-size apples (about 1¼ pounds), peeled and thinly sliced

2 teaspoons freshly squeezed lemon juice

½ teaspoon grated lemon zest

½ cup (55 grams) chopped pecans, toasted

¼ cup (40 grams) raisins

¼ cup (55 grams) brown sugar

1 teaspoon cinnamon

½ teaspoon kosher salt

For the dough

1 (17.3-ounce) package store-bought puff pastry, thawed

2 tablespoons matzo meal or bread crumbs

For the egg wash and topping

1 large egg

1 teaspoon water

1 teaspoon granulated or coarse sugar (optional)

1. **Make the filling:** In a medium bowl, combine the sliced apples, lemon juice, and zest. Add the pecans, raisins, brown sugar, cinnamon, and salt and mix well.

2. **Preheat/Prep:** Preheat the oven to 375°F. Line a baking sheet with parchment paper; then temporarily move the parchment paper to the work surface for rolling. Unroll the thawed puff pastry onto the parchment paper. With a rolling pin, roll it out to a 12-by-16-inch rectangle, with the short edge closest to you.

3. **Fill and shape:** Sprinkle the matzo meal on just the bottom half of the puff pastry, leaving a 1-inch border. Lay the apple filling over the matzo meal, leaving a 1-inch border near the bottom and side edges. Roll the puff pastry up like a log from the short edge; then place it seam-side down and tuck the loose sides under. Transfer the parchment paper with the strudel back to the baking sheet.

4. **Egg wash:** In a small bowl, whisk together the egg and water to make an egg wash. Brush the egg wash over the exterior of the puff pastry. Use a sharp knife to cut 3 or 4 diagonal slits in the top of the strudel to release steam. Sprinkle the strudel with granulated sugar (if using).

5. **Bake:** Bake the strudel for 30 minutes, until the pastry is golden brown and juices are bubbling. Let cool on the baking sheet for at least 10 minutes before slicing. Transfer the strudel to a wire rack to help retain its crispy bottom, but do so carefully so you don't burn yourself or break the strudel. Eat a slice when it's still warm!

Ingredient Tip: Puff pastry should be completely thawed (but not warm) before you unroll it, or it might crack at the folds. If it becomes too warm and difficult to handle while rolling out or forming the strudel, return it to the refrigerator, uncovered, for a few minutes to chill before continuing.

Traditional Potato and Cheese Borekas

PREP TIME: 1 hour 15 minutes • **COOK TIME:** 50 minutes

"Boreka" comes from the Turkish word borek, meaning pie. Doughs and fillings vary dramatically by region. In Israel, borekas feature puff pastry, and popular fillings include cheese, eggplant, and mushrooms. In Turkey, borek are usually made with phyllo dough and are filled with meat, cheese, spinach, and herbs. This recipe is a traditional Sephardic boreka, with an oil-based dough and a potato-and-cheese filling. You can just picture all the aunts and grandmas gathered around the table, making them by the hundreds for a special occasion. ✳ MAKES 30 TO 36 BOREKAS

For the filling

1 pound (454 grams) russet potatoes, peeled, chunked

8 ounces (245 grams) feta cheese (preferably in brine, not pre-crumbled)

2 ounces (25 grams) grated Parmesan or Romano cheese

½ teaspoon white pepper or 1 teaspoon grated lemon zest (optional)

2 large eggs, beaten

For the dough

1 cup (235 grams) hot water (120°F to 130°F)

1 cup (224 grams) vegetable oil

1 teaspoon kosher salt

5 cups (625 grams) all-purpose flour, divided

1. **Prep:** In a medium saucepan filled with salted water, boil the potatoes for 15 to 20 minutes, until fork-tender. Drain. (Alternatively, place in a microwaveable bowl and steam in the microwave with no water for about 6 minutes.) Line 2 baking sheets with parchment paper.

2. **Mix:** While the potatoes are cooking, make the dough. In a large bowl, whisk together the hot water, oil, and salt. Add 4 cups of flour and combine with a wooden spoon. Add the remaining 1 cup of flour, ¼ cup at a time, until the dough comes together and "feels like an earlobe," as tradition describes it. Knead the dough a few times in the bowl to be sure all the flour is incorporated; then cover the bowl with a kitchen towel and let the dough rest while you make the filling.

3. **Make the filling:** In a medium bowl, mash the potatoes. Crumble the feta into the bowl, and add the Parmesan and the white pepper or lemon zest (if using). Mix well. Taste and adjust seasonings; then mix in the 2 beaten eggs.

**For the egg wash
and topping**

1 large egg

1 teaspoon water

Sesame seeds (optional)

**Grated Parmesan
or Romano cheese
(optional)**

Variation Tip: Try the traditional rope fold. After sealing the boreka shut, place it in your hand and use the thumb and index finger of your other hand to pinch and push, pinch and push along the seal. You'll see a scalloped, ropelike pattern emerge.

4. **Preheat:** Preheat the oven to 375°F. If you plan on baking both sheets at once, adjust the oven racks to the top and bottom thirds of the oven.

5. **Fill and shape:** Take a walnut-size piece of dough, roll it into a ball, and place it on an un-floured work surface. (The dough is very oily and will not stick.) Use your palm to flatten the dough and roll it into a 4-by-3-inch oval. Place a heaping tablespoon of the filling just below the midpoint of the oval. Flatten the filling just a bit and fold the dough over, creating a half-moon shape. Press the edges together, and use the tines of a fork to crimp shut, forming a seal. Place on one of the prepared baking sheets and repeat with remaining dough and filling.

6. **Egg wash:** In a small bowl, whisk together the egg and water. Brush each boreka with the egg wash and sprinkle with sesame seeds or Parmesan (if using).

7. **Bake:** Bake for 30 minutes, or until golden brown and crispy. If using 2 baking sheets at once, rotate the sheets halfway through baking. Enjoy warm, and store leftovers in the refrigerator for up to 3 days or the freezer for 3 months. Reheat in the oven at 325°F: 10 minutes to reheat, and 20 to 25 minutes from frozen.

Make-ahead Tip: To prepare borekas in advance, freeze them before baking and bake straight from the freezer. If frozen, just add a few extra minutes in the oven.

Pastelicos, Meat-Filled Borekas

PREP TIME: 1 hour • **COOK TIME:** 45 minutes

Fill a boreka with meat, and it becomes a pastelle or pastelico. The meat filling always includes ground beef and onion, and often rice. I've added pine nuts for texture and parsley for color. This version veers from tradition by using store-bought puff pastry. If you're feeling fancy, you can use this filling with the homemade dough from Traditional Potato and Cheese Borekas (page 54). Bonus points if you learn the traditional pastelico bowl-shaped dough form, topped with a pastry "hat" and finished with sesame seeds. ✴ MAKES 18 PASTELICOS

For the filling

1 medium onion,
  finely chopped
2 tablespoons olive oil
1 pound (454 grams)
  ground beef
1 teaspoon paprika
1 tablespoon plus
  1 teaspoon lemon juice
½ cup (30 grams) parsley,
  finely chopped
⅓ cup (36 grams) pine
  nuts, toasted
1 teaspoon kosher salt
½ teaspoon black pepper
1 large egg, beaten

For the dough

1 (17.3-ounce) package
  store-bought puff
  pastry, defrosted but
  kept chilled

1. **Make the filling:** In a large skillet over medium heat, sauté the onion in the olive oil, stirring frequently, for 3 to 5 minutes, until it begins to brown. Push the onion to one side of the pan and add the ground beef. Brown the meat, breaking it up into smaller pieces and mixing it around as it continues to cook, another 5 to 7 minutes. When the beef is almost cooked, add the paprika, lemon juice, parsley, pine nuts, salt, and pepper, and mix. Taste for seasoning and set aside to cool. Once the filling is cooled, add the beaten egg and mix well.

2. **Preheat:** Preheat the oven to 375°F. Line 2 baking sheets with parchment paper. If you plan on baking both sheets at once, adjust the oven racks to the top and bottom thirds of the oven.

3. **Prep the pastry:** On a lightly floured surface roll out the puff pastry to a roughly 12-by-12-inch square. Using a pizza cutter, cut the pastry into 9 equal-size squares. Refrigerate the squares, lightly covered with a towel, while you repeat with the second piece of pastry. If at any point in the process the puff pastry gets warm, put it in the refrigerator to chill before proceeding.

For the egg wash and topping

1 large egg

1 teaspoon water

2 tablespoons sesame seeds

4. **Fill and shape:** Spoon 2 tablespoons of filling onto a pastry square, near a corner, leaving a small border for crimping. Fold the pastry in half diagonally to make a triangle. Using the tines of a fork, crimp the edges closed. Place the pastelico on one of the prepared baking sheets. Repeat with the rest of the squares. Keep the shaped pastelicos refrigerated and repeat the process with the remaining filling and puff pastry.

5. **Egg wash:** In a small bowl, whisk together the egg and water. Brush each pastry with the egg wash and sprinkle with the sesame seeds. Place both baking sheets in the refrigerator for 10 minutes, uncovered, to chill the pastelicos.

6. **Bake:** Bake the pastelicos for 25 to 30 minutes, until they are puffed and golden brown. If using 2 baking sheets at once, rotate the sheets halfway through. Cool for a few minutes, then enjoy warm.

Orange–Olive Oil Hamantaschen

PREP TIME: 1 hour • **INACTIVE TIME:** 1 hour to overnight • **COOK TIME:** 25 minutes

I have fond memories of my grandmother's hamantaschen, the 3-sided triangular cookies traditionally eaten on Purim. My brothers and I especially loved the little cookies she would make with extra scraps of dough. I re-created her oil-based hamantaschen using a mild extra-virgin olive oil. Nobody will complain when these arrive in their mishloach manot care package.

MAKES 20 TO 24 HAMANTASCHEN

For the dough

2½ cups (313 grams)
   all-purpose flour

1½ teaspoons cornstarch

½ teaspoon kosher salt

1 teaspoon baking powder

¼ teaspoon baking soda

½ cup (94 grams)
   granulated sugar

Grated zest of 1 orange

¼ cup (62 grams) orange
   juice (from zested orange)

1 large egg

⅓ cup (70 grams)
   extra-virgin olive oil

1 teaspoon vanilla

For the egg wash

1 large egg

1 teaspoon water

1. **Mix:** In a medium bowl, whisk together the flour, cornstarch, salt, baking powder, and baking soda. In another medium bowl, combine the sugar and orange zest, using your fingers to rub the zest into the sugar. To this sugar mixture, add the orange juice, egg, oil, and vanilla and whisk until combined.

2. **Form the dough:** Add the wet mixture to the dry mixture and stir until it forms a thick dough. Use your hands to knead the dough a few times, just until it comes together. The dough may be a bit wet.

3. **Rest:** Form the dough into 2 equal balls, wrap each in plastic wrap, and refrigerate for at least 30 minutes or overnight.

4. **Prep:** Line 2 baking sheets with parchment. In a small bowl, beat the egg and water to make an egg wash.

5. **Make the filling:** Place the prunes in a small pot, and just cover them with water. Bring to a boil over medium heat. Once the water reaches a boil, turn the heat to low and simmer for 5 to 7 minutes, until the prunes soften. Using a slotted spoon, transfer the prunes to a mixing bowl or a mini food processor, reserving the prune water. Add the orange zest and juice, sugar, and 2 teaspoons of prune water. Mash with a fork or pulse until

For the filling

4 ounces prunes (about 12)

½ cup (118 grams) water (or to cover)

Zest of ½ orange

2 teaspoons freshly squeezed orange juice

1 tablespoon granulated sugar

3 teaspoons reserved prune water, divided

¼ cup (29 grams) chopped toasted walnuts (optional)

combined—a few larger chunks of prune are okay. Taste for flavor, and if the filling seems thick, add one more teaspoon of the prune water. Stir in the nuts (if using).

6. **Roll out the dough:** Remove 1 dough ball from the refrigerator and roll it between 2 sheets of parchment paper to about ⅛- to ¼-inch thick, as thinly as you can without tearing it. The shape you roll can be oblong—the dough's thickness is more important.

7. **Fill and shape:** Use a 2½- or 3-inch round cookie cutter to cut out 20 to 24 circles total and place them on the prepared baking sheets. Brush each circle with egg wash, then place a teaspoon of filling in the center. Use your thumbs and forefingers to cinch the dough into a triangle, creating 3 corners and firmly pinching them closed, leaving a hole for the filling to peek through.

8. **Preheat:** Preheat the oven to 350°F. If you plan to bake both sheets at once, adjust the oven racks to the top and bottom thirds of the oven.

9. **Chill:** While the oven preheats, return the cookies to the refrigerator for 15 to 30 minutes. This will help the cookies retain their shape.

10. **Egg wash:** Brush the exterior of the cookies with more of the egg wash.

11. **Bake:** Bake the hamantaschen for about 18 minutes, until light golden brown. If using 2 baking sheets at once, rotate the sheets halfway through baking. Transfer the cookes to a wire rack to cool before serving.

Hermine's Hamantaschen

PREP TIME: 1 hour • **INACTIVE TIME:** 1 hour 30 minutes • **COOK TIME:** 15 minutes

When my friend Sharon offered me her mother's butter-based hamantaschen recipe, my eyes lit up. Hermine was a prolific baker, whose cookies have lived on past her time on this earth. I fell in love with the pure charm of her recipe even before I tasted the cookies themselves—for instance, the original instructions say, "Add half an eggshell of orange juice." For this book's purposes, I've turned that gem into a more standard measurement and added my own touch of salt and fragrant lemon zest. ✶ MAKES 24 HAMANTASCHEN

For the dough

¾ cup
(1½ sticks/170 grams)
unsalted butter, room
temperature

¾ cup (141 grams)
granulated sugar

3 cups (375 grams)
all-purpose flour, plus
more for shaping

2 teaspoons
baking powder

½ teaspoon kosher salt

2 large eggs, beaten

1 teaspoon grated
lemon zest

⅛ cup freshly squeezed
orange juice

For the filling

½ cup prune filling,
from Orange–Olive Oil
Hamantaschen (page 58)

For the egg wash

1 large egg

1 teaspoon water

1. **Cream the butter:** To the bowl of a stand mixer fitted with the paddle attachment, add the butter and sugar. Cream on medium-low speed for about 2 minutes, until light and fluffy.

2. **Mix:** Add the flour, baking powder, and salt and mix on low speed to combine. Add the beaten eggs, lemon zest, and orange juice. Continue mixing on low speed for about 1 minute, until the mixture comes together in a ball of dough.

3. **Rest:** Divide the dough into 4 equal pieces, wrap in plastic wrap, and refrigerate for at least 1 hour.

4. **Prep and egg wash:** While the dough is resting, line 2 baking sheets with parchment paper. In a small bowl, whisk together the egg and water to make an egg wash.

5. **Roll out the dough:** Remove 1 ball of dough from the refrigerator. On a well-floured surface, pat the ball into a disk. Flour the top and use a rolling pin to roll the dough to ⅛-inch thick. Check that the dough lifts easily off the surface (and won't stick) by gently moving it with a bench scraper or your hands.

Filling the hamantaschen

6. **Fill and shape:** Use a 3-inch or 2½-inch round cookie cutter to cut out as many circles as you can and place them on the prepared baking sheets. Using a pastry brush, brush each circle with the prepared egg wash and place a scant teaspoon of filling in the center. Use your thumbs and forefingers to cinch the dough into a triangle, creating 3 corners and firmly pinching them closed, leaving a hole for the filling to peek through. You can also combine the scraps and re-roll one time as well. (Or just bake them like my bubbe did.) Repeat with the remaining dough.

7. **Preheat:** Preheat the oven to 375°F. If you plan to bake both sheets at once, adjust the oven racks to the top and bottom thirds of the oven.

8. **Chill:** While the oven preheats, return the cookies to the refrigerator for 15 to 30 minutes. This will help ensure the cookies retain their shape during baking.

9. **Egg wash:** Remove from the refrigerator and brush each cookie with more egg wash.

10. **Bake:** Bake at 375°F for 15 minutes, until light golden brown. If using 2 baking sheets at once, rotate the sheets halfway through baking. Transfer the cookies to a wire rack and cool before serving.

Variation Tip: Use other fillings such as homemade or store-bought jams, traditional poppy seed filling, or even a crowd favorite, hazelnut spread.

Blintz Casserole

PREP TIME: 25 minutes • **COOK TIME:** 50 minutes

When Shavuot or Yom Kippur arrives, you'll be ready to go with this deconstructed blintz casserole. Almost soufflé-like but far easier to make, you'll feed a crowd without worrying about the time it would otherwise take to make individual blintzes. This comes together in a 9-by-13-inch casserole pan (or 2 deep-dish pie pans). Serve slices topped with Berry Fruit Compote (page 110), and your need for brunch, a meal to break the fast, or late-night Shavuot snacks is solved! ✴ SERVES 10 TO 12

For the batter

2 tablespoons unsalted butter, melted, plus more for greasing the pan

4 large eggs

½ cup (118 grams) water

1 cup (244 grams) whole or low-fat milk

¼ cup (61 grams) Greek yogurt

¼ cup (62 grams) freshly squeezed orange juice

2 teaspoons baking powder

1¾ cups (219 grams) flour

½ teaspoon kosher salt

For the filling

6 ounces (170 grams) cream cheese, softened

1 cup (226 grams) cottage cheese (drained)

2 cups (496 grams) ricotta or farmer cheese (drained)

1. **Preheat/Prep:** Preheat the oven to 350°F. Grease a 9-by-13-inch baking pan with butter.

2. **Mix:** In a blender, combine the eggs, water, milk, yogurt, orange juice, melted butter, baking powder, flour, and salt on medium-high speed. Refrigerate the batter to let it rest while you make the cheese filling.

3. **Make the filling:** In a medium bowl, combine the cream cheese, cottage cheese, ricotta, eggs, sugar, vanilla, and lemon zest with a wooden spoon or hand mixer.

4. **Assemble the casserole:** Pour half the batter into the prepared baking pan and bake for 7 to 8 minutes, until just set. Carefully remove the pan from the oven and pour the cheese mixture over the just-set batter, partially blocking it with the back of a wooden spoon so it lands softly. Spread the cheese mixture over the whole bottom layer. Gently spoon the remaining batter on top of the cheese filling—it's okay if the batter seeps into the cheese mixture.

2 large eggs

3 tablespoons
granulated sugar

1 teaspoon vanilla

1 teaspoon grated
lemon zest

Berry Fruit Compote
(page 110), for serving

5. **Bake:** Return the pan to the oven for 35 to 40 minutes, until the casserole feels set in the middle. Set the oven to broil and broil for 1 to 2 minutes, to brown the top. Cool slightly and serve with Berry Fruit Compote.

Make-ahead Tip: This casserole reheats very nicely, making it easy to prep for a brunch or holiday gathering. Just pop it in the oven at 350°F until crisped up and heated through.

Apricot Chocolate Rugelach

PREP TIME: 1 hour • **INACTIVE TIME:** 2 hours 30 minutes to overnight • **COOK TIME:** 35 minutes

Rugelach is a rolled pastry featuring a rich butter, cream cheese, and sour cream dough. In Israel, the dough is yeast-based and finished with a shiny sweet glaze. Though they're not tied to a specific holiday, our family happens to make rugelach for Hanukkah. Our recipe was originally inspired by a recipe in a 1990 *Food & Wine* magazine, but, over the years, these little gems have become our family calling card. ★ MAKES 48 RUGELACH

For the dough

1 cup (2 sticks/227 grams) unsalted butter, room temperature

4 ounces (116 grams) cream cheese, room temperature

½ cup (115 grams) sour cream, room temperature

2 tablespoons (25 grams) granulated sugar

1¾ cups (218 grams) all-purpose flour

For the filling

¾ cup (105 grams) semi-sweet mini chocolate chips or chopped dark chocolate

¾ cup (88 grams) walnuts, toasted and finely chopped

¼ cup (36 grams) currants

1. **Cream the butter:** In the bowl of a stand mixer fitted with the paddle attachment, add the butter and cream cheese. Cream on medium speed until soft and creamy, about 1 minute. Add the sour cream and sugar and continue to mix until well combined, about 1 minute.

2. **Mix:** Turn the speed to low. Add the flour to the mixture in 2 batches, mixing to incorporate until the dough forms.

3. **Form the dough:** Transfer the dough to a piece of parchment paper and divide it into 4 equal pieces. Pat each piece into a disk, wrap in plastic wrap, and refrigerate for at least 2 hours, overnight, or even a few days (or freeze for up to 2 months).

4. **Make the filling:** In a medium bowl, combine the chocolate, walnuts, currants, cinnamon, and sugar. Set aside. (Make ahead or combine right before you roll the rugelach.)

5. **Roll out the dough:** Remove 1 dough piece from the refrigerator. On a lightly floured surface, roll the dough into a circle about 10 inches in diameter and ⅛ inch thick.

1 teaspoon cinnamon

2 tablespoons (25 grams) granulated sugar

¾ cup (240 grams) apricot preserves

6. **Fill:** Spread 2 tablespoons of apricot preserves over the dough. If the preserves are too thick, add a little water, microwave to room temperature (not warm), and mix to loosen preserves slightly. Sprinkle ½ cup of filling mixture evenly over the dough and press it in gently. (The cinnamon sugar falls to the bottom of the mixture, so scoop from the bottom of the bowl.)

7. **Prep:** Line 2 baking sheets with parchment paper.

8. **Shape:** Using a pizza cutter or knife, cut the dough round into 12 long triangles. Starting at the wide end of a triangle, roll the dough tightly, but carefully, toward the point, as you would a croissant. Place the rugelach on the prepared baking sheet, pointed-side down. Repeat with the remaining triangles, arranging them about ½ inch apart. Repeat steps 5 through 8 with the remaining dough, preserves, and filling mixture. Once all the rugelach are formed, brush the tops with more apricot preserves.

9. **Chill:** As each pan of rugelach is completed, pop it in the refrigerator to chill for 30 minutes, uncovered. It will help them bake without flopping open.

10. **Preheat:** While the rugelach are chilling, preheat the oven to 350°F. If you plan to bake both baking sheets at once, adjust the oven racks to the top and bottom thirds of the oven.

CONTINUED ▸

11. **Bake:** Transfer the baking sheets from the refrigerator directly to the oven and bake for 30 to 35 minutes, or until well browned, rotating the baking sheets halfway through. Let the rugelach rest on the baking sheet for a few minutes before transferring them to a wire rack to cool thoroughly before serving (they actually taste even better once cooled).

Storage Tip: If tightly wrapped, baked rugelach can be frozen for up to 3 months. Return to room temperature before serving. I recommend making a double batch to enjoy year-round.

Make-ahead Tip: This recipe can be divided into shorter, easier stages: Make the dough one day, the filling the next, and roll, form, and bake the third day.

Sally's Baklava

PREP TIME: 1 hour • **INACTIVE TIME:** 10 minutes • **COOK TIME:** 50 minutes

Baklava, a layering of delicate phyllo pastry with nuts and syrup, is a crunchy delight. "Phyllo" is Greek for "leaf," and premade "leaves" are available in the frozen section of most grocery stores. My friend's mom, Sally Benveniste, a Sephardic Jew from Salonika, Greece, taught me to make baklava years ago. She simplifies how the butter is applied, a technique she learned from the original newspaper-clipped recipe. Sally changed the syrup to her family version; I've added some optional aromatics and increased the amount of walnut filling. ✳ MAKES 24 TO 28 SQUARES

For the filling

4 cups (400 grams) walnuts, toasted

½ cup (94 grams) granulated sugar

1 tablespoon cinnamon

½ teaspoon nutmeg

For the syrup

1 cup (188 grams) granulated sugar

½ cup (121 grams) water

½ cup (170 grams) honey

1 tablespoon freshly squeezed lemon juice

1 cinnamon stick (optional)

2 strips orange rind (optional)

For the dough

1 cup (2 sticks/227 grams) unsalted butter, melted

1 (16-ounce) package store-bought phyllo (filo), thawed

1. **Make the filling:** In the food processor, combine the walnuts, sugar, cinnamon, and nutmeg and process until the mixture looks like sand and small pebbles. Transfer the mixture to a medium bowl and set aside.

2. **Make the syrup:** In a small saucepan, combine the sugar, water, honey, lemon juice, cinnamon stick (if using), and orange rind (if using). Bring to a boil over medium heat, reduce the temperature to low, and simmer for 5 minutes. Let the syrup cool until you are ready to use it.

3. **Preheat/Prep:** Preheat the oven to 350°F. Near a flat work surface, place a 9-by-13-inch baking dish, a pastry brush, and the melted butter. Gently lay the phyllo on the work surface and trim the sheets into 8-by-12-inch rectangles to fit the baking dish. Cover the phyllo with plastic wrap *and* a kitchen towel to prevent it from drying out.

CONTINUED ▸

Variation Tip: The syrup
is a good place to adjust
flavors. Try using cardamom,
rose water, or orange blossom water (tread lightly with
the waters; use ½ teaspoon
at a time). You can also
substitute pistachios for
half of the walnuts. The key
with baklava is to learn the
technique before bending
the flavors to your liking.

4. **Assemble the baklava:** Brush melted butter on
the bottom of the pan. Add the phyllo, 2 sheets at
a time, drizzling with butter after every 2 sheets.
When you get to the 15th sheet, add ⅓ of the filling
(about 1 cup), spreading it all over the surface.
Then add 5 more phyllo sheets, drizzling butter
after every 2 and adding the filling to the 5th.
Repeat the 5 layers of phyllo and butter and add
another cup of filling. You may have some filling
left over. Finish the layering as you started with
15 more layers of phyllo, buttering after every 2.
Do not butter the top layer.

5. **Score:** To cut the baklava, use a very sharp knife
and cut all the way through the layers. You can keep
it simple and make 24 squares, or cut each square
into a diamond. If this is your first time making
baklava, start with squares to get used to cutting
the phyllo. If any butter remains, spoon it into the
cut lines.

6. **Bake:** Bake the cut baklava for about 45 minutes,
checking it at 40 minutes. The top should be
brown, and you should hear it bubbling.

7. **Add the syrup:** Let the baklava cool for 5 minutes;
then use a spoon to drizzle the syrup into all of the
cuts. Depending on your sweet tooth, you might
use all the syrup or have a little left over. Allow the
baklava to cool completely before enjoying. You
can refrigerate the baklava for up to 2 weeks or
freeze for up to 2 months.

Grandma Mellman's Knishes

PREP TIME: 1 hour • **COOK TIME:** 1 hour

When I announced I was writing a cookbook, my friend Jay told me I had to talk to his brother Kenny. According to Jay, Kenny made Grandma's knishes, and they couldn't be beat. Like many old recipes, words were sparse, and Kenny had added in touches from the current generation. (One tip mentioned to "roll them up like a sushi roll.") When I described knishes to my husband, he likened them to omusubi, a Japanese rice ball. Despite the creative analogies, this classic comfort food will take you back to an old-world Jewish deli, complete with spicy mustard for dunking. ✳ MAKES 24 KNISHES

For the filling

2 large or 3 medium
   onions, finely chopped
2 tablespoons olive oil
6 tablespoons
   (¾ stick/85 grams)
   unsalted butter, room
   temperature, divided
2½ pounds russet pota-
   toes, peeled, cut into
   2-inch chunks
1 teaspoon kosher salt
2 teaspoons black pepper

For the dough

4 cups (500 grams)
   all-purpose flour
1 teaspoon baking powder
1 teaspoon kosher salt
⅓ cup (74 grams)
   vegetable oil
2 large eggs
1 cup (235 grams) warm
   water (105°F to 115°F)

1. **Sauté:** In a large skillet, sauté the onions in the olive oil and 2 tablespoons of butter over medium-low heat for 5 minutes. When the onions begin to sizzle, reduce the heat to low and continue cooking the onions until translucent and beginning to brown, 15 to 20 more minutes.

2. **Cook the potatoes:** While the onions cook, bring a large pot of salted water to a boil. Add the potatoes and boil until tender, about 15 minutes, and drain. Alternatively, microwave the potatoes until fork tender, about 6 minutes. Set aside.

3. **Make the dough:** In a large bowl, whisk together the flour, baking powder, and salt. In a medium bowl, whisk together the oil, eggs, and water. Add the liquid mixture to the flour mixture and stir with a wooden spoon until a rough dough comes together. Transfer the dough to a floured work surface and knead until smooth and tacky but not sticky. Cover with plastic wrap or kitchen towel and let it rest for at least 15 minutes while you finish the filling.

CONTINUED ▶

¼ cup (½ stick/57 grams) unsalted butter, melted and cooled to room temperature (for rolling the dough)

For the egg wash
1 large egg
1 teaspoon water

4. **Make the filling:** In a medium bowl, mash the cooked potatoes with the remaining 4 tablespoons of butter. If the potatoes are not hot enough to melt the butter, melt the butter in the microwave before adding it to the potatoes. Add the salt, pepper, and sautéed onions. Mash until well incorporated and taste for seasoning.

5. **Preheat/Prep:** Preheat the oven to 375°F. Line 2 baking sheets with parchment paper. If you plan to bake both sheets at once, adjust the oven racks to the top and bottom thirds of the oven. In a small bowl, beat the egg and water to make an egg wash.

6. **Roll out dough:** Divide the dough in half and lightly dust a work surface with flour. Roll out the first half of the dough as thinly as you can without tearing, into a 20-by-10-inch rectangle.

7. **Fill and roll dough:** Brush the surface of the dough with the cooled melted butter. Spread half of the potato mixture along the long edge closest to you, leaving a 2-inch border. Starting with the long edge closest to you, roll the dough up into a log. Stretch the dough up and over the filling and continue rolling. If the dough feels stuck to the work surface, use a plastic dough scraper to help it along.

8. **Shape the knishes:** Once it is rolled up, place the dough log seam-side down. Cut the log into about 2-inch segments. Pinch each segment closed on one side. On the other side, either stretch the dough up to partially cover the filling or pull the dough up and twist it fully closed. Shape the knishes to be wider and flatter as needed. Place the knishes on the prepared baking sheets. Repeat steps 6 through 8 with the remaining dough and filling.

9. **Bake:** Use a pastry brush to brush the outside of each knish with the prepared egg wash. Bake for 30 minutes, or until golden brown. If using 2 baking sheets at once, rotate the sheets halfway through baking. Serve warm.

Pecan and Raisin Schnecken

PREP TIME: 30 minutes • **INACTIVE TIME:** 2 to 3 hours • **COOK TIME:** 25 minutes

Jewish bakers from Germany brought schnecken (meaning "snails" in German) to the United States. Once you cut these cinnamon-roll-like pastries, you'll see the resemblance. Over the years, many cookbooks have updated their schnecken, calling them cinnamon buns or even sticky buns. My recipe is not exactly either—this dough is made with melted butter, resulting in a sturdy pastry that encases the pecans and raisins perfectly in individual muffin-tin portions. ✱ MAKES 12 BUNS

For the dough

3 cups (375 grams)
  all-purpose flour

2¼ teaspoons
  (7 grams/1 packet)
  active dry yeast or
  instant yeast

¼ cup (47 grams)
  granulated sugar

½ cup (1 stick/114 grams)
  unsalted butter, melted

½ cup (122 grams) warm
  milk (105°F to 115°F)

1 teaspoon kosher salt

1 large egg

For the filling

1 cup (220 grams)
  brown sugar

2 teaspoons cinnamon

¼ teaspoon kosher salt

¾ cup (120 grams) raisins

1½ cups (164 grams)
  pecans, toasted and
  coarsely chopped

½ cup (1 stick/114 grams)
  unsalted butter, melted

1. **Mix:** In the bowl of a stand mixer, whisk together the flour, yeast, and granulated sugar. In a small bowl, mix the melted butter, warm milk, and salt, making sure the temperature is between 105°F and 115°F. Add the milk mixture to the dry ingredients, along with the egg.

2. **Knead:** Using the stand mixer fitted with the dough hook attachment, begin kneading the mixture on low speed to combine. After about 1 minute, turn up the speed to medium and continue kneading for about 5 minutes, until the dough feels soft and slightly tacky but not sticky.

3. **First rise:** Form the dough into a ball, place it in a medium bowl, cover with plastic wrap, and set it aside to rise for 2 to 3 hours. It should almost double in size.

4. **Make the filling:** While the dough is rising, in a medium bowl, mix the brown sugar, cinnamon, salt, raisins, and pecans.

5. **Prep:** Generously grease a 12-cup muffin tin with some of the melted butter. Spoon 2 teaspoons of the brown sugar filling into each tin.

6. **Roll out the dough:** Transfer the dough onto the work surface (no need to flour it because of the butter in the dough). Using your hands, begin to flatten it and form it into a rectangle. With a rolling pin, roll it into a 12-by-18-inch rectangle. Brush more of the melted butter over the dough, leaving a ½-inch border along the longer edges.

7. **Fill and roll the buns:** Spread the remaining brown sugar filling over the dough. Starting at the long edge closest to you, roll the dough into a log. If the edges are ragged, trim them. Cut the log into 12 buns, each about 1½ inches wide. Place each bun cut-side up in one of the muffin tin cups and brush the tops with more melted butter.

8. **Second rise:** Cover the buns with plastic wrap and let them rise for about an hour. They won't double in size, but the dough should become softer and somewhat puffy.

9. **Preheat:** While the buns are rising, preheat the oven to 375°F.

10. **Bake:** Bake the schnecken for 20 to 25 minutes, until the internal temperature reaches at least 190°F and the tops are nicely browned. Let the buns cool for a few minutes. Place a large serving tray or baking sheet on top of the muffin tin and quickly invert it. The buns should pop out with the layer of pecans and raisins on top. If any of the filling stuck to the muffin cups, scoop it out onto the buns. Serve warm.

CHAPTER FOUR

Cookies and Cakes

◄ Sandy's Poppy Seed Coffee Cake

Biscochos de Benveniste

PREP TIME: 1 hour • **INACTIVE TIME:** 20 to 30 minutes • **COOK TIME:** 35 minutes

It seems like every region has its own all-purpose, barely sweet cookie/cracker of some sort. Ashkenazim have kichel, Mizrahim have ka'ak, and Sephardim have biscochos. Even within a single family, there are variations on the ingredients or process. In my friend Sally Benveniste's family, for instance, one person adds cinnamon to their biscochos and slowly reduces the oven temperature. Another person omits the cinnamon and bakes at a single temperature. The hallmark of these twice-baked cookies is their notched, circular shape. Variations aside, as Sally says, "I always have a jar of biscochos in my kitchen." ✳ MAKES 30 COOKIES

For the batter

4 large eggs

1 cup (188 grams) granulated sugar

½ cup (112 grams) vegetable oil

1 teaspoon vanilla extract

4 to 4¼ cups (500 to 531 grams) all-purpose flour, divided

1 tablespoon plus 1 teaspoon baking powder

½ teaspoon cinnamon

½ teaspoon kosher salt

For the egg wash and topping

1 large egg

1 teaspoon water

¼ cup sesame seeds, optional

Cinnamon sugar (1 teaspoon cinnamom, 3 teaspoons granulated sugar) (optional)

1. **Whisk:** In a large bowl, whisk together the eggs until well combined and frothy. Add the sugar, oil, and vanilla and whisk again to combine.

2. **Mix dough:** Add 2 cups of flour, the baking powder, cinnamon, and salt to the egg mixture and mix with a wooden spoon. Then add another 2 cups of flour and mix well. The dough should feel tacky, not sticky, and easy to knead and roll. If it's extremely sticky, add another ¼ cup of the remaining flour and use your hands to incorporate it.

3. **Knead:** Transfer the dough to a floured work surface and knead it a few times. Once it is a bit oily but no longer sticky, cover the dough by turning the bowl upside down over it and let it rest for 20 to 30 minutes.

4. **Preheat/Prep:** Preheat the oven to 350°F. Line 2 baking sheets with parchment paper. If you plan to bake both sheets at once, adjust the oven racks to the top and bottom thirds of the oven.

5. **Roll the dough:** Divide the rested dough into roughly 8 pieces. Keep the dough pieces covered so they don't dry out. On an un-floured surface, use the palms of your hands to roll the dough ball into a long, thin rope. It should be about ½ inch in diameter and between 30 and 35 inches long. Using a paring knife, make angled notches halfway through the rope every ⅓ inch or so. At 12 notches, you should have a rope about 4 to 5 inches long. Cut the rope and repeat.

6. **Form the cookies:** Take a rope and connect its ends to create a loop. Place it on the prepared baking sheet. Repeat with half of the dough, which should fill 2 baking sheets.

7. **Egg wash:** Whisk the egg and water together to create an egg wash. Brush each cookie with the egg wash and top the cookies with sesame seeds and/or cinnamon sugar (if using).

8. **Bake:** Bake the cookies for 20 minutes. If using 2 baking sheets at once, rotate the sheets halfway through baking. Turn the oven off and remove the trays to cool for 5 minutes.

9. **Second bake:** Return the 2 trays to the turned-off oven to bake a second time, for about 15 minutes. They won't look much different, but they'll be even crispier. Let cool completely on the parchment or a cooling rack before storing. Repeat steps 6 through 9 with the other half of the dough. If you want to bake half one day and half the next, the dough will keep in the refrigerator tightly wrapped for a day or two.

Nana's Mandelbrot

PREP TIME: 20 minutes • **INACTIVE TIME:** 1 hour to overnight • **COOK TIME:** 50 minutes

Mandelbrot, which in Yiddish means almond bread, is a twice-baked cookie that visually resembles the better-known Italian biscotti, though its higher fat content makes it a bit softer and less brittle. I based this recipe on my friend's special recipe collection that she inherited from her Nana. If you think of mandelbrot as a dry, tasteless, overcooked biscuit, give these a try—one of my tasters said she would buy this book just for this recipe. ✳ MAKES 36 COOKIES

For the batter

3 cups (375 grams)
all-purpose flour

2 teaspoons
baking powder

1 teaspoon kosher salt

¾ cup (168 grams)
vegetable oil

3 large eggs

½ teaspoon almond
extract (optional)

1 teaspoon vanilla extract

1 cup (188 grams)
granulated sugar

1 tablespoon grated
orange zest

½ cup (80 grams) dried
cherries

½ cup (47 grams) chopped
almonds, toasted

For the topping

4 tablespoons granulated
sugar (optional)

1 tablespoon cinnamon
(optional)

1. **Mix:** In a medium bowl, whisk together the flour, baking powder, and salt. In another medium bowl, vigorously whisk together the oil, eggs, almond extract (if using), vanilla, sugar, and orange zest until pale lemon-yellow in color and frothy.

2. **Form the dough:** Add roughly ¾ of the flour mixture to the egg mixture and use a wooden spoon to mix thoroughly. To the remaining flour mixture, add the dried cherries and almonds and toss to coat them with flour. Add the fruit, almond, and flour mixture into the dough and stir until no flour is visible.

3. **Chill:** Cover with plastic wrap and refrigerate the dough for at least an hour or even overnight.

4. **Preheat/Prep:** Preheat the oven to 350°F. Line 2 baking sheets with parchment paper. If you plan to bake both sheets at once, adjust the oven racks to the top and bottom thirds of the oven.

5. **Shape:** Place the chilled dough on a well-floured work surface and divide in half. Form each piece into a rectangular log roughly 12 inches long, 2 inches wide, and 1 inch tall. Place 1 log on each baking sheet. The logs will spread when baked, so don't try to fit both on one baking sheet.

6. **First bake:** Bake for 30 minutes, rotating the baking sheets halfway through. Remove the baking sheets from the oven and cool for 15 minutes. Remove the mandelbrot from the baking sheets by picking up the parchment paper and place them on a surface safe for slicing; then lower the oven temperature to 250°F.

7. **Slice:** Line the same baking sheets with fresh parchment paper. In a small bowl, combine the cinnamon and sugar for the topping (if using). Once the logs have cooled, use a serrated knife to slice them at an angle (for longer pieces) or straight across horizontally (for smaller ones).

8. **Second bake:** Place the cut cookies flat on the prepared baking sheets. Sprinkle with the cinnamon sugar (if using). Bake for an additional 20 minutes, rotating the baking sheets halfway through. Cool to room temperature before serving. Store leftovers in an airtight container for up to a week.

Substitution Tip: Swap out the almonds for hazelnuts, pecans, pistachios, or walnuts. Or, switch out the dried cherries for cranberries, golden raisins, or currants. You could also substitute or add chocolate chips.

Chocolate-Dipped Almond Coconut Macaroons

PREP TIME: 20 minutes • **INACTIVE TIME:** 1 hour to overnight • **COOK TIME:** 20 minutes

These macaroons might not look familiar if, like me, you grew up eating canned macaroons at Passover. My macaroons don't have a homogeneous texture, nor are they cloyingly sweet. They crisp up on the outside but stay soft and chewy inside, and I use unsweetened coconut to help temper the sweetness. For a variation, bake some before chilling the batter, and you'll have a macaroon shaped like a cookie. ✳ MAKES 22 TO 24 COOKIES

For the batter

2 egg whites

½ teaspoon kosher salt

¾ cup (141 grams) granulated sugar

¾ cup (60 grams) unsweetened shredded coconut

1 cup (120 grams) almond flour

½ teaspoon almond extract

½ teaspoon vanilla extract

For the topping

¾ cup (170 grams/6 ounces) semisweet or bittersweet chocolate, chopped (chocolate chips are okay)

1. **Preheat/Prep:** Preheat the oven to 350°F. Line 2 baking sheets with parchment paper. If you plan to bake both sheets at once, adjust the oven racks to the top and bottom thirds of the oven.

2. **Whip:** In the bowl of a stand mixer fitted with the whisk attachment, whip the egg whites on high speed until soft peaks form. Add the salt, and begin slowly adding the sugar, ¼ cup at a time. Continue whipping until the whites are shiny, silky, and form stiff peaks, or until tracks in the whites don't quickly disappear.

3. **Mix the batter:** Remove the bowl from the stand mixer. Using a rubber spatula, gently fold in the coconut, almond flour, almond extract, and vanilla.

4. **Shape:** If you prefer traditional, tall macaroons, refrigerate the batter for at least an hour (or overnight) before scooping tablespoons of macaroon batter onto the prepared baking sheets. If you prefer flatter, cookie-like macaroons, scoop tablespoons of un-chilled batter directly onto the prepared baking sheets, leaving about 2 inches of space between scoops to allow for spreading.

5. **Bake:** Bake the macaroons at 350°F for 15 to 17 minutes, until they are slightly golden brown on top and the middles are just turning firm. If using 2 baking sheets at once, rotate the sheets halfway through baking. Use a toothpick to check doneness. Cool completely.

6. **Dip:** In the microwave, melt the chocolate in 30-second increments, stirring with a wooden spoon after each increment. Mix vigorously until the chocolate is fully melted and looks shiny. Dip each macaroon, covering half of the cookie (or dipping only the tops). Place dipped macaroons on parchment paper to allow the chocolate to set. Once the chocolate sets, store in an airtight container for up to 5 days.

Variation Tip: Try these cookies without the chocolate—you may decide they need no embellishment. You can also add mini chocolate chips into the batter before baking for a slightly different take.

Date and Walnut Thumbprints

PREP TIME: 50 minutes • **INACTIVE TIME:** 2 hours 45 minutes to overnight
COOK TIME: 35 minutes

This cookie is a variation on a Persian cookie, kloocheh, in Louisa Shafia's *The New Persian Kitchen*. As Shafia explains, kloocheh appear in many forms along the Silk Road and in religions from Buddhism to Judaism. I modified this recipe by making it into a thumbprint cookie. These gems are perfect for Purim Tu B'shevat or Rosh Hashanah. ★ MAKES 24 COOKIES

For the dough

2 cups (250 grams) all-purpose flour

½ teaspoon kosher salt

1 teaspoon ground cardamom

2 teaspoons baking powder

1 cup (2 sticks/227 grams) unsalted butter, room temperature

⅓ cup (62 grams) granulated sugar

1 teaspoon vanilla extract

1 large egg

2 teaspoons grated orange zest

1. **Whisk:** In a medium bowl, whisk together the flour, salt, cardamom, and baking powder.

2. **Cream the butter:** In the bowl of a stand mixer fitted with the paddle attachment, cream together the butter and sugar on medium-high speed for about 3 minutes, until light and fluffy. Add the vanilla, egg, and orange zest and mix on medium speed until just combined.

3. **Mix the dough:** Reduce the mixer speed to low and add the flour mixture to the butter mixture in 2 batches, stopping to scrape down the sides of the bowl as needed. This recipe makes a firm dough, so you may need to use your hands to incorporate the last bit of flour.

4. **Rest:** Transfer the dough to a piece of plastic wrap, press it into a disk, and wrap it. Chill in the refrigerator for 2 hours, until firm but still flexible. (You can also refrigerate it overnight.)

5. **Make the filling:** In a small saucepan, combine ¼ cup of walnuts, the dates, cinnamon, orange juice, honey, and salt and bring to a boil over medium heat. Lower the heat and simmer, uncovered, for 5 to 7 minutes, stirring often until the mixture forms a thick paste. Transfer the paste to a bowl and let cool to room temperature.

For the filling

½ cup (59 grams)
finely chopped
walnuts, divided

½ cup (60 grams)
Medjool dates, pitted
and chopped

½ teaspoon cinnamon

¼ cup (62 grams) freshly
squeezed orange juice

2 teaspoons honey

¼ teaspoon kosher salt

¼ cup (30 grams)
powdered
sugar, for dusting

Variation Tip: For a lovely, complex flavor profile, replace the orange zest with 2 teaspoons of orange blossom water and 1 teaspoon of rose water—the flavors pair well with the cardamom in the cookie and the orange in the filling. You can find both of these ingredients online or at a local Middle Eastern market.

6. **Form cookies:** Line 2 baking sheets with parchment paper. To make a thumbprint cookie, wet your hands and break off a walnut-size piece of dough. Roll the dough into a ball and flatten it with the palm of your hand to about ½ inch thick. Place on a baking sheet and use your thumb to make an indent in the center. Repeat with the remaining dough.

7. **Fill cookies:** Fill the indents in the dough with ½ teaspoon each of the date mixture and sprinkle some of the remaining walnuts on top.

8. **Chill:** Refrigerate the cookies for 45 minutes, uncovered, until firm.

9. **Preheat:** While the cookies chill, preheat the oven to 350°F. If you plan to bake both sheets at once, adjust the oven racks to the top and bottom thirds of the oven.

10. **Bake:** Bake the cookies for about 25 minutes, until just beginning to brown, and golden on the undersides. If using 2 baking sheets at once, rotate the sheets halfway through baking. Transfer to a wire rack and cool completely. Dust the cooled cookies with the powdered sugar and serve. Store in an airtight container at room temperature for up to 5 days.

Black-and-White Cookies

PREP TIME: 45 minutes • **COOK TIME:** 25 minutes

As a former East Coast Jew, I'm embarrassed to admit I never ate black-and-white cookies. When I confessed this to cookbook author Emily Paster, she joked, "Are you even Jewish?" It's only fitting that Emily, who has strong opinions on what an authentic black-and-white cookie should be, influenced this recipe. I've shared her icing recipes because she told me in no uncertain terms, "My recipe is *exactly* what they should taste like." ✳ MAKES 12 TO 14 COOKIES

For the batter

2 cups (250 grams)
   all-purpose flour

1 teaspoon baking powder

¼ teaspoon baking soda

½ teaspoon kosher salt

½ cup (1 stick/113 grams)
   unsalted butter, room
   temperature

¾ cup (141 grams)
   granulated sugar

1 teaspoon grated
   lemon zest

2 large eggs, room
   temperature

2 teaspoons vanilla extract

⅓ cup (81 grams) Greek
   yogurt or sour cream,
   room temperature

Nonstick cooking spray

1. **Preheat/Prep:** Preheat the oven to 375°F. Line 2 baking sheets with parchment paper. Adjust the oven rack to the center shelf.

2. **Mix:** In a medium bowl, whisk together the flour, baking powder, baking soda, and salt.

3. **Cream the butter:** In the bowl of a stand mixer fitted with the paddle attachment, cream together the butter, sugar, and lemon zest on medium-high speed for about 4 minutes, until light and fluffy. Scrape down the sides of the bowl. Add the eggs and vanilla and continue to beat on medium-high speed until well combined, about 1 minute.

4. **Mix the batter:** Reduce the speed to low and slowly add the flour mixture and the yogurt, starting and ending with the dry mixture and alternating between the two, until just combined. Scrape down the sides of the bowl as necessary.

5. **Scoop the cookies:** Spray a ¼-cup measuring cup with nonstick cooking spray. Scoop ¼ cup of batter onto the baking sheet, up to 6 cookies per sheet. Use an offset spatula to flatten each cookie to about ½ inch thick, keeping it as circular as possible. Use nonstick spray on the spatula to prevent sticking.

For the icings

2½ cups (300 grams)
   powdered sugar, sifted
4 to 5 tablespoons
   (76 grams to 91 grams)
   whole milk, divided
1 tablespoon corn syrup
½ teaspoon vanilla extract
¼ cup (22 grams)
   unsweetened cocoa
   powder, sifted

6. **Bake:** Bake the cookies one sheet at a time on the center rack for 11 to 12 minutes. The cookies will spread and puff up, and the underside will be golden brown. Transfer to a wire rack to cool while you prepare the icing.

7. **Prepare the white icing:** In a medium bowl, whisk together the powdered sugar, 2 tablespoons of milk, the corn syrup, and the vanilla. Your icing should be thick but pourable—add another table-spoon of milk if needed.

8. **Spread the white icing:** Using an offset spatula or knife, spread the white icing on half of **the flat side** of each cooled cookie. Place the iced cookies on the cooling rack and let the icing harden, 5 to 10 minutes.

9. **Prepare the chocolate icing:** After you've iced half of each cookie with white icing, stir the cocoa powder and 1 tablespoon of milk into the remain-ing white icing to create the chocolate icing. If the icing is too thick, add another tablespoon of milk—it should have a thick but spreadable consistency.

10. **Spread the chocolate icing:** Ice the other half of the cookie, starting by making a line down the middle as straight as you can and then covering the rest of the cookie. Let the icing harden again, another 5 to 10 minutes.

11. **Store:** Store the cookies in an airtight container for 2 to 3 days—but be sure to eat one immediately.

Crispy Bow-Tie Kichel

PREP TIME: 30 minutes • **INACTIVE TIME:** 30 minutes • **COOK TIME:** 25 minutes

If your memory of kichel conjures up the image of a stale Oneg Shabbat cookie platter, I don't blame you—but please overwrite that reference by making these cookies. Though rolled in sugar, they're actually not too sweet—there's little sugar in the dough itself. According to *The World of Jewish Desserts* by Gil Marks, kichel were traditionally served alongside savory herring or egg salad. Good kichel are light as air, which explains their other moniker: *sweet nothings*. With their adorable bow-tie shape, don't blame me if you fall in love with this crispy treat. ✴ MAKES 5 TO 6 DOZEN COOKIES

For the dough

2 cups (250 grams) all-purpose flour

1 teaspoon baking powder

1 teaspoon kosher salt

4 large eggs

1 tablespoon granulated sugar, plus ¾ cup (141 grams) for rolling, divided

½ cup (112 grams) vegetable oil

1 teaspoon vanilla extract

For the topping

Cinnamon sugar (¼ teaspoon cinnamon, 1 teaspoon granulated sugar) (optional)

1 tablespoon sesame seeds (optional)

1. **Preheat/Prep:** Preheat the oven to 350°F. Line 2 baking sheets with parchment paper. If you plan to bake both sheets at once, adjust the oven racks to the top and bottom thirds of the oven.

2. **Mix the dough:** In a medium bowl, whisk together the flour, baking powder, and salt. In the bowl of a stand mixer fitted with the paddle attachment, beat the eggs, 1 tablespoon of sugar, the oil, and vanilla on medium-low speed about 1 minute, until smooth and lemony yellow. Add the flour mixture and mix on low speed for 1 minute until combined. Turn the speed back up to medium-low and continue mixing for another 8 to 10 minutes, stopping to scrape down the sides of the bowl if necessary. The dough will be very sticky. Cover the bowl with a kitchen towel or plastic wrap and let the dough rest for 30 minutes.

3. **Roll out the dough:** On a clean work surface or piece of parchment paper, pour out ½ cup of the remaining sugar and spread it into a roughly 13-by-13-inch square. Using a plastic dough scraper, transfer the dough from the bowl to the sugared surface. Pour the remaining ¼ cup of

sugar on top of the dough. Roll the dough out to a roughly 13-by-13-inch square, to fill the area with the sugar. The dough should be ¼-inch thick. If needed, it's okay to sprinkle more sugar on the dough while rolling it out.

4. **Form the cookies:** Using a pizza cutter, cut the dough into 1-by-2-inch pieces (odd shapes on the ends are fine). Pick up a piece of cut dough (use a bench scraper to help if need be), twist it into a bow, twist it again, and place it on the prepared baking sheet. Repeat with all of the dough. Sprinkle the cookies with cinnamon sugar or sesame seeds (if using).

5. **Bake:** Bake the kichel for 25 minutes, rotating the baking sheets halfway through. The cookies should be nicely browned and puffed, and the sugar should have formed cracked patterns. Let cool completely before storing in an airtight container. Cookies will stay fresh for at least a week at room temperature, and can also freeze well for up to 2 months.

Marble Pound Cake

PREP TIME: 40 minutes • **COOK TIME:** 45 minutes

Whether you want a non-fried, oil-based dessert for Hanukkah or a nice loaf cake to serve at brunch, or just love a toasted slice of pound cake with a cup of coffee, this marble pound cake suits any and every dessert need. Marbling adds minimal extra work but offers a visually striking result that never fails to impress. It's also a great nostalgic treat for those of us who grew up eating a certain store-bought brand of marble cake. ✳ SERVES 6 TO 8 PEOPLE

Nonstick cooking spray

3 tablespoons unsweet-
ened cocoa powder

3 tablespoons, plus 1 cup
(188 grams) granulated
sugar, divided

2 tablespoons water

2 cups (250 grams)
all-purpose flour, plus
more for dusting pan

1½ teaspoons
baking powder

1 teaspoon kosher salt

½ cup (107 grams) olive oil

1 teaspoon vanilla extract

3 large eggs, room
temperature

½ cup (122 grams)
unsweetened almond
milk, room temperature

1. **Preheat/Prep:** Preheat the oven to 325°F. Spray an 8½-by-4½-inch loaf pan with nonstick cooking spray and dust it with flour. If using a larger 9-by-5-inch loaf pan, reduce the baking time by 5 minutes.

2. **Mix:** In a medium bowl, stir together the cocoa powder, 3 tablespoons of sugar, and the water to form a thick paste. Set aside. In a separate medium bowl, whisk together the flour, baking powder and salt.

3. **Mix batter:** In the bowl of a stand mixer fitted with the paddle attachment, beat the remaining 1 cup of sugar, the oil, and vanilla for 2 to 3 minutes on medium-high speed. Add the eggs one at a time, and beat for 1 minute on medium-high speed after each addition. Reduce the speed to low and slowly add the flour mixture and almond milk, starting and ending with the dry mixture and alternating between the two, until fully combined.

4. **Make the chocolate batter:** Remove about 1 cup of batter and stir it into the bowl with the cocoa powder paste mixture.

5. **Marble the batter:** Spoon each batter into the prepared loaf pan in alternating layers. Once all the batter is in the pan, take a knife or tooth-pick and zigzag it down the pan, making about 6 strokes, to "marbleize" the loaf. Don't overdo it, or you'll have a homogeneous cake.

6. **Bake:** Bake the loaf for about 45 minutes, or until a toothpick comes out clean. Let the pan cool on a wire rack for 15 minutes, then remove the cake from the pan and continue to cool to room temperature.

Apple Cake with Candied Ginger and Cinnamon

PREP TIME: 20 minutes • **COOK TIME:** 55 minutes

Versatility is this cake's middle name. It was originally adapted from a Marian Burros plum cake recipe. Then, the blog *Kosher Camembert* adapted it into an apple cake recipe. Then I turned it into a pear cake recipe for my own blog. For this book, I decided to use Rosh Hashanah's featured fruit and take it back to apple cake—but if you want to color outside the lines, use pears or plums instead. ✷ SERVES 8 TO 10 PEOPLE

For the batter

2 cups (220 grams) apples, peeled, cored, and cut into 1-inch dice (about 2 medium apples)

Juice of ½ lemon

2 cups (250 grams) all-purpose flour

2 teaspoons baking powder

½ teaspoon kosher salt

1 teaspoon cinnamon

3 large eggs

½ cup (94 grams) granulated sugar

½ cup (110 grams) brown sugar

¾ cup (174 grams) extra-virgin olive oil (mild flavor), plus more for greasing the pan

2 teaspoons vanilla

1 to 2 tablespoons chopped crystallized candied ginger

1. **Preheat/Prep:** Preheat the oven to 350°F. Line the bottom of a 9-inch round cake pan (springform if possible) with parchment paper, and grease the sides of the pan with olive oil. In a small bowl, place the diced apples for the batter, and in another bowl the sliced apples for the topping. Sprinkle the lemon juice evenly over each bowl to prevent browning. Set aside.

2. **Whisk:** In a medium bowl, whisk together the flour, baking powder, salt, and cinnamon. In another medium bowl, whisk together the eggs, granulated sugar, and brown sugar for about 1 minute. Add the oil and vanilla to the egg mixture and whisk again.

3. **Mix the batter:** Add the flour mixture to the egg mixture and combine with a wooden spoon. Add the diced apples and ginger and mix again.

4. **Pour:** Pour the batter into the prepared pan. Decorate the top with the sliced apples in a circular pattern. In a small bowl, mix together the granulated sugar and cinnamon and sprinkle over the apples.

For the topping

**1 apple, peeled, cored, and
sliced thinly**

**¾ teaspoon granu-
lated sugar**

¼ teaspoon cinnamon

5. **Bake:** Bake the cake for 50 to 55 minutes until the top of the cake is golden brown and a toothpick comes out clean. Let cool for 10 to 15 minutes. Release the outside of the springform pan and carefully place the cake on a serving platter. Cool before serving.

Make-ahead Tip: You can wrap this cake tightly in plastic wrap and aluminum foil and freeze it for up to 2 months.

Sandy's Poppy Seed Coffee Cake

PREP TIME: 30 minutes • **INACTIVE TIME:** 1 hour • **COOK TIME:** 55 minutes

I was thrilled when my friend Susan shared her treasured coffee cake recipe, written on a stained index card more than 60 years ago by her dear friend Sandy. It's a versatile treat—transporting me back to Brooklyn, acting as a "bribe" to help my friend reduce rush charges for her business, and providing a soothing snack for her ailing friend. My sister-in-law also makes a legendary coffee cake, so I added cocoa powder to the streusel to pay homage to her chocolate-studded version. ✳ SERVES 12 TO 14

For the batter

⅓ cup (49 grams) poppy seeds

1 cup (244 grams) buttermilk

Nonstick cooking spray

2½ cups (313 grams) all-purpose flour

1 teaspoon baking soda

2 teaspoons baking powder

1 teaspoon kosher salt

4 large eggs, separated, room temperature

1 cup (2 sticks/227 grams) unsalted butter, room temperature

1½ cups (282 grams) granulated sugar

1 teaspoon vanilla extract

1. **Soak:** In a small bowl or 2-cup liquid measuring cup, soak the poppy seeds in the buttermilk for 1 hour.

2. **Make the filling:** In a medium bowl, mix together the walnuts, brown sugar, granulated sugar, cinnamon, and cocoa powder. Set aside.

3. **Preheat/Prep:** Preheat the oven to 350°F. Generously grease a 9½-inch Bundt pan with nonstick cooking spray.

4. **Sift:** In a medium bowl, sift together the flour, baking soda, baking powder, and salt.

5. **Whip:** In the bowl of a stand mixer fitted with the whisk attachment, whip the egg whites for about 2 minutes on medium-high speed, to form stiff peaks. Transfer to another bowl and set aside

6. **Cream the butter:** Using the stand mixer fitted with the paddle attachment, cream the butter and granulated sugar for 3 to 5 minutes on medium speed until fluffy. Add the egg yolks and vanilla and continue to mix on medium speed until combined, about 1 to 2 more minutes. Scrape the sides of the bowl as needed.

For the filling

¾ cup walnuts (88 grams), chopped and toasted

½ cup (110 grams) brown sugar

¼ cup (47 grams) granulated sugar

1 tablespoon cinnamon

1 tablespoon unsweetened cocoa powder

7. **Mix:** Adjust the speed to low and slowly add the flour mixture and buttermilk poppy seed mixture, starting and ending with the flour and alternating between the two until all are incorporated.

8. **Fold the batter:** Remove the bowl from the stand mixer and fold in the egg whites using a rubber spatula. The batter will be very thick once you add the poppy seed mixture so it will take a minute or two to incorporate the egg whites fully.

9. **Pour:** Pour ⅓ of the batter into the greased Bundt pan. Add ½ of the streusel filling, then another ⅓ of the batter, then the other ½ of the streusel filling. Finish with the last of the batter. Use a spatula to help spread the thick batter.

10. **Bake:** Bake for 50 to 55 minutes until golden brown and a toothpick comes out clean. Start checking for doneness at 45 minutes. Carefully remove from the Bundt pan after cooling for 10 minutes.

Honey Kovrizhka, Russian Honey Cake

PREP TIME: 35 minutes • **COOK TIME:** 1 hour

This recipe comes from my friend Vera's Jewish grandma Riva, who was born in Poland and eventually settled in Zhitomir (now Ukraine). Her grandma would pull the cake from an ancient chest in the kitchen, tightly wrapped in linen cloth. Vera vividly remembers the scents of honey, ginger, and cinnamon, ingredients not available in Vera's region of Russia. This cake tastes even better 5 to 7 days after you bake it and can be stored for up to a month. ✳ SERVES 24

1 cup (237 grams) strong brewed black tea, strained

1 cup (339 grams) honey

1 cup (188 grams) granulated sugar (brown sugar is also okay)

⅓ cup (74 grams) vegetable oil

1 teaspoon baking soda

½ teaspoon cinnamon

1 teaspoon ground ginger

½ teaspoon ground nutmeg

½ teaspoon ground cloves

Nonstick cooking spray

3 large eggs

3 to 3¼ cups (375 grams to 406 grams) all-purpose flour

1 cup (117 grams) chopped walnuts, toasted

½ cup (73 grams) raisins

1. **Boil the tea mixture:** In a large pot, add the freshly brewed tea, honey, sugar, and oil. Bring the mixture to a boil over medium-high heat, stirring until the honey and sugar dissolve. Turn the heat to medium and add the baking soda. Keep stirring for another 30 seconds. The mixture will foam and expand in volume. Add the cinnamon, ginger, nutmeg, and cloves and mix. Set the mixture aside and let it cool to room temperature.

2. **Prep/Preheat:** Preheat the oven to 350°F. Grease a 9½-inch Bundt pan with nonstick cooking spray.

3. **Mix the batter:** Once the tea mixture has cooled, add the eggs and mix well with a whisk. Add 3 cups of flour, 1 cup at a time, whisking in between additions. As the dough becomes thicker, switch to a wooden spoon. The batter should be the consistency of a thick but pourable milkshake. If it seems too thin, add the final ¼ cup of flour. When the batter is smooth and thick, stir in the walnuts and raisins.

4. **Bake:** Pour the batter into the prepared Bundt pan. With a spatula, smooth the batter. Bake for 45 to 50 minutes. Depending on the color and size of the Bundt pan, the bake time could be up to 1 hour. If a toothpick comes out clean or the internal temperature is above 190°F, it is ready.

5. **Store:** Place the Bundt pan on a cooling rack. When the cake reaches room temperature, release it from the pan and wrap it in a kitchen towel. The flavor of the honey and spice will evolve over time, so this cake is even better after a day or two—but I won't stop you having a slice right out of the oven.

Flourless Chocolate Cake with Jam-Liqueur Sauce

PREP TIME: 30 minutes • **COOK TIME:** 30 minutes

What makes a flourless chocolate cake a "Jewish" dessert? Well, no flour and no leavening makes it perfect for Passover, so Jews can have their chocolate cake and eat it, too. Dress this up with fresh fruit, ice cream, or whipped cream, or make my quick jam sauce with your choice of liqueur, from Cointreau to amaretto to crème de menthe. ✶ SERVES 10 TO 12

For the batter

Nonstick cooking spray

10 ounces (283 grams) semisweet or bittersweet chocolate, chopped (or use high-quality chips)

¾ cup (1½ sticks/170 grams) unsalted butter, cut into ½-inch cubes, room temperature

1 cup (188 grams) granulated sugar

5 large eggs

2 tablespoons sweet Passover wine, port, or liqueur of your choice (optional)

½ teaspoon kosher salt

¼ cup (24 grams) unsweetened cocoa powder, sifted

For the sauce

½ cup (160 grams) jam of choice

2 tablespoons liqueur of choice

1. **Preheat/Prep:** Preheat the oven to 350°F. Grease a 9-inch springform pan with nonstick cooking spray and line the bottom of the pan with a parchment paper round.

2. **Melt the chocolate:** In a small bowl, microwave the chocolate and butter on high, in 30-second increments, mixing after each increment. When the chocolate and butter are almost melted, stir vigorously to finish the melting. Set aside to cool.

3. **Beat:** In the bowl of a stand mixer, whisk the sugar and eggs until the color lightens and they appear fluffy, about 2 minutes. Add the Passover wine (if using), the salt, and the sifted cocoa powder, and continue whisking until thoroughly incorporated. (You can complete this step by hand as well.)

4. **Mix the batter:** Add ⅓ of the chocolate-butter mixture and whisk until incorporated. Repeat with the remaining chocolate mixture, working in thirds, until fully combined.

5. **Bake:** Pour the batter into the prepared spring-form pan. Bake for 30 minutes. The center should be almost set, and the edges should have begun to pull away from the pan. Cool for at least an hour, then remove the springform pan and carefully transfer the cake to a serving platter. Store at room temperature until ready to serve.

6. **Make the sauce:** In a small bowl, microwave the jam and liqueur for 15 seconds. Mix, taste, and adjust by adding more jam or liqueur to taste. Cool the sauce to room temperature before serving.

7. **Serve:** Drizzle the sauce on top of each slice of cake, or serve on the side.

Make-ahead Tip: The cake and sauce can be made a day ahead. Store the cake on the counter under a cake dome or in plastic wrap, and store the sauce, covered, in the refrigerator. Leftovers are good for 2 to 3 days at room temperature; refrigerate after that. The cake also freezes surprisingly well for up to a month when wrapped tightly in plastic wrap and foil.

New York–Style Cheesecake Bars

PREP TIME: 25 minutes • **INACTIVE TIME:** 6 hours to overnight • **COOK TIME:** 55 minutes

New York–Style cheesecake is known for its high volume of cream cheese and just a hint of lemon. It's not a light bite, but it has a rich and pleasing mouthfeel. This simple-to-make cheesecake dessert is perfect for Shavuot, when eating dairy products is traditional. My bars are far easier to make than a round cheesecake in a springform pan, which requires a water bath. Enjoy this luscious treat anytime you need an easy, make-ahead dessert option. ✳ MAKES 16 BARS

For the crust

Nonstick cooking spray
10 graham crackers
(yield about 1¾ cups
of crumbs)
6 tablespoons (85 grams)
unsalted butter, melted
2 tablespoons brown sugar
¼ teaspoon kosher salt

For the filling

16 ounces (464 grams)
cream cheese, room
temperature
½ cup (94 grams)
granulated sugar
2 large eggs, room
temperature
½ cup (123 grams) Greek
yogurt or sour cream
(115 grams), room
temperature
2 teaspoons vanilla extract
2 tablespoons freshly
squeezed lemon juice
1 teaspoon grated
lemon zest
¼ teaspoon kosher salt
1 tablespoon flour

1. **Prep/Preheat:** Preheat the oven to 350°F. Line an 8-by-8-inch pan with aluminum foil, leaving an overhang on two opposite sides. Spray the foil lightly with nonstick cooking spray.

2. **Make the crust:** Use a food processor or a rolling pin and a plastic bag to crush the graham crackers to a fine crumb. Transfer the crumbs to a small bowl and stir in the melted butter, brown sugar, and salt. Mix well so the crumbs are coated with butter. Transfer the graham cracker crust to the foil-lined pan and press down firmly with your fingers or the bottom of a glass. The crust should cover the bottom of the pan and extend up the sides of the pan by about 1 inch. Bake for 8 minutes. Remove from the oven to cool slightly before adding the filling.

3. **Make the filling:** Lower the oven temperature to 325°F. In the bowl of a stand mixer fitted with the paddle attachment, cream together the cream cheese and granulated sugar on medium speed for about 1 minute, until well combined. Scrape down the sides of the bowl and add the eggs, yogurt, vanilla, lemon juice, lemon zest, salt, and flour. Mix well on medium speed for another 1 minute. Pour the filling into the cooled crust.

4. **Bake:** Bake for 40 to 45 minutes, checking at 40 minutes. The cheesecake should be mostly set, with the middle still a bit jiggly. Let cool for 30 minutes and refrigerate for 6 hours or overnight. To serve, use the foil overhang to lift it out of the pan onto a cutting board. Slice into squares, wiping the knife clean in between each cut. Enjoy as is, or top with fruit, jam, or whipped cream.

Variation Tip: Use a mini muffin pan and mini muffin liners. Place about 1 tablespoon of crust in each liner, pressing down with the bottom of a shot glass. Bake crusts for 5 minutes at 350°F. Remove and cool. Add a heaping tablespoon of filling and bake for 18 to 20 minutes.

Light-as-Air Tishpishti

PREP TIME: 45 minutes • **COOK TIME:** 40 minutes

Tishpishti means "quickly cooked cake" in Turkish. I've chosen to make it Passover-friendly by using almond flour, but semolina and regular flour are popular choices for this cake as well. Because of the honey syrup, this cake is also perfect for Rosh Hashanah. No matter the flour or the holiday, all tishpishti cakes include a flavored syrup (think baklava), orange flavor, and, most commonly, walnuts. ✳ MAKES 24 SQUARES

For the syrup

1 cup (235 grams) water

1 cup (188 grams) granulated sugar

2 tablespoons freshly squeezed lemon juice

3 strips lemon rind

3 strips orange rind

Cinnamon stick

For the batter

1½ cups (176 grams) toasted walnuts

Nonstick cooking spray

5 large eggs, separated, room temperature

¾ cup (141 grams) granulated sugar

⅓ cup (71 grams) extra-virgin olive oil

⅓ cup (82 grams) freshly squeezed orange juice

1 teaspoon grated orange zest

1½ cups (168 grams) almond flour

2 teaspoons cinnamon

1. **Make the syrup:** In a medium saucepan, boil the water, sugar, lemon juice, lemon rind, orange rind, and cinnamon stick over medium-high heat. Reduce the heat to low and simmer for 10 minutes to slightly thicken and reduce the liquid. Set the syrup aside to cool while you make the cake.

2. **Prep/Preheat:** Finely chop the walnuts. Preheat the oven to 350°F. Grease a 9-by-13-inch baking pan with nonstick cooking spray. Line the pan with a parchment liner, allowing an inch or two of overhang to help remove the cake from the pan, unless you plan to serve it directly from the pan.

3. **Beat:** In the bowl of a stand mixer fitted with the paddle attachment, beat the egg yolks and sugar on medium-high speed for about 2 minutes, until the egg mixture is pale yellow. Add the oil, orange juice, and orange zest, and continue beating for another minute on medium-high speed. Add the walnuts, almond flour, and cinnamon and reduce the speed to low. Beat until just incorporated and transfer to another bowl. Wash and dry the bowl of the stand mixer.

4. **Whip:** Using the stand mixer fitted with the whisk attachment, whip the egg whites on high speed until they form stiff peaks, 1 to 2 minutes.

5. **Fold the batter:** Gently fold a cup of the whipped egg whites into the batter to soften it up; then fold in the rest of the whites until evenly incorporated.

6. **Bake:** Pour the batter into the prepared pan and bake for 30 minutes. Let the cake cool for about 5 minutes, then gently slice it into squares or diamonds. If you are not serving the cake directly from the pan, transfer it to a serving platter. Pour ¾ to 1 cup of syrup over the cake. Serve warm, at room temperature, or chilled. You can store this cake in the refrigerator for up to a week.

Citrus Sponge Cake

PREP TIME: 45 minutes • **COOK TIME:** 50 minutes

When I was growing up, boxed Passover sponge cake was on regular rotation every Pesach. One year, I was brave enough to make one from scratch, only to watch it deflate in defeat. Learn from my past mistakes and make this recipe instead. Cool it upside down and I promise you'll have a light, pillowy sponge cake filled with the fresh scent of lemon and orange. And be sure to note that this recipe uses matzo *cake* meal, not regular matzo meal. ✳ SERVES 10 TO 12

½ cup (80 grams) matzo cake meal

1 cup (192 grams) potato starch

½ teaspoon kosher salt

6 large eggs, room temperature, separated

1½ cups (282 grams) granulated sugar, divided

2 tablespoons freshly squeezed orange juice

3 tablespoons freshly squeezed lemon juice

1 teaspoon grated orange zest

1 teaspoon grated lemon zest

Whipped cream, for serving (optional)

Berry Fruit Compote (page 110), (optional) for serving

1. **Preheat/Prep:** Preheat the oven to 325°F. When the cake comes out of the oven, you'll need to cool it in the pan upside down, so you'll need a 10-inch tube cake pan with a removable bottom. Check if the tube pan can balance upside down on its own. (If it can't, find the neck of a bottle on which it can balance.)

2. **Sift:** In a medium bowl, sift together the cake meal, potato starch, and salt.

3. **Mix:** In the bowl of a stand mixer fitted with the paddle attachment, beat the egg yolks on high speed for 1 minute. Gradually add ¾ cup of sugar and continue to beat until the mixture is thick and pale yellow, about 3 minutes more. Scrape down the sides of the bowl if needed. Add the orange juice, lemon juice, orange zest, and lemon zest and beat on medium speed to combine. Add the matzo cake meal mixture to the egg mixture and beat on low speed for about 1 more minute. Move the mixture to a large bowl. Wash and dry the bowl of the stand mixer.

4. **Whip:** Using the stand mixer fitted with the whisk attachment, beat the egg whites on high speed until soft peaks form, about 2 minutes. Add the remaining ¾ cup of sugar, ¼ cup at a time, and beat until the whites are thick, stiff, and glossy, about 2 more minutes.

5. **Fold the batter:** Fold a cup of the egg whites into the yolk mixture to soften up the mixture; then fold in the remaining egg whites. Pour the batter into the ungreased tube pan.

6. **Bake:** Bake the cake for 45 to 50 minutes. It will nearly double in volume and should be golden brown.

7. **Cool:** Cool the cake for an hour by turning the entire tube pan upside down, balancing the tube on the neck of a wine bottle if necessary.

8. **Release:** Once completely cool, turn the pan right-side up, slip a knife around the edge of the cake to release it, and carefully lift the center tube (and thereby the cake). To separate the cake from the tube piece, use a flat spatula to lift up the bottom of the cake from the bottom of the pan. Carefully lift the cake up and transfer it to a serving platter. Serve with whipped cream and Berry Fruit Compote (if using).

Honey Cookies

PREP TIME: 30 minutes • **INACTIVE TIME:** 30 minutes • **COOK TIME:** 15 minutes

Known as duvshaniot (Hebrew for "small honeyed cookies"), these bite-size morsels are a lovely addition to Rosh Hashanah gift baskets. To let the honey flavor shine, I've kept the spice level moderate and added some citrus for brightness. This simple-to-make treat is delightful with a cup of tea or coffee.

MAKES 48 COOKIES

2½ cups (313 grams) all-purpose flour

¼ teaspoon baking soda

1 teaspoon baking powder

½ teaspoon kosher salt

1 teaspoon cinnamon

½ teaspoon ginger

½ teaspoon nutmeg

2 large eggs

½ cup (1 stick/114 grams) unsalted butter, melted

½ cup honey

¼ cup (55 grams) brown sugar

1 tablespoon freshly squeezed lime juice

1 teaspoon grated lime zest

½ cup (94 grams) granulated sugar

Kosher Tip: To make Pareve honey cookies, use ¼ cup plus 2 tablespoons of vegetable oil or olive oil in place of the butter.

1. **Mix:** In a medium bowl, whisk the flour, baking soda, baking powder, salt, cinnamon, ginger, and nutmeg. In another medium bowl, vigorously whisk the eggs, melted butter, honey, brown sugar, lime juice, and lime zest.

2. **Form the dough:** Add the flour mixture to the egg mixture and combine with a spatula or wooden spoon until you see no visible flour.

3. **Chill:** Cover the bowl with plastic wrap and chill the dough in the refrigerator for 30 minutes.

4. **Preheat/Prep:** Preheat the oven to 350°F. Line 2 baking sheets with parchment. If you plan to bake both sheets at once, adjust the oven racks to the top and bottom thirds. Place the granulated sugar in a shallow bowl.

5. **Roll the cookies:** Once the dough is chilled, take heaping tablespoon-size pieces and roll into 1-inch balls. Roll the dough balls in the sugar and place them on the baking sheets, about 2 inches apart. Using your hands or the tines of a fork, flatten the cookies until they are about ¼-inch thick.

6. **Bake:** Bake the cookies for 10 to 12 minutes, until they have spread and begin to brown on the undersides. If using 2 baking sheets at once, rotate the sheets halfway through baking. Transfer to wire racks to cool.

CHAPTER FIVE

More Treats and Toppings

◂ Baked or Fried Soufganiyot (Jelly Donuts)

Marilyn's Pestila

PREP TIME: 20 minutes • **INACTIVE TIME:** 1 hour • **COOK TIME:** 1 hour 5 minutes

I've known my friend Sarene since grade school, but I recently learned that her mom's family came from a region in China called Harbin, where Russian Jews lived during the late 19th through the mid-20th centuries. From that little-known former Jewish enclave comes a specialty courtesy of her mom, Marilyn. Made with prunes, it's called Pestila (Pastilla), and it's absolutely delicious—think of it as a cross between a jelly bean, jam, and nougat. Pestila makes a sweet addition to Passover desserts and snacks. Pair with chocolate or cheese for a delicious combination. ✦ MAKES 4 LOGS

For the prune mixture

2 cups (234 grams)
  walnuts, toasted

1 pound (454 grams)
  pitted prunes

1½ cups (282 grams)
  granulated sugar

½ cup (170 grams) honey

1 tablespoon plus
  1 teaspoon freshly
  squeezed lemon juice

½ teaspoon cinnamon

**For the matzo
meal coating**

¼ cup (30 grams)
  matzo meal

¼ teaspoon cinnamon

¾ teaspoon
  granulated sugar

¼ teaspoon kosher salt

1. **Prep:** Finely chop the walnuts.

2. **Toast the matzo meal coating:** In a small skillet, toast the matzo meal, cinnamon, sugar, and salt over medium heat for about 5 minutes. Watch it carefully and keep stirring with a wooden spoon. As soon as it begins to brown, it's done. Transfer the mixture to a plate to cool.

3. **Make the prune mixture:** In the bowl of a food processor, grind the prunes to a paste for about 30 seconds. They will still have some texture. In a medium saucepan, combine the prunes and sugar. Cover the pan and cook over very low heat until the sugar dissolves, about 30 minutes. Stir every few minutes to ensure the bottom isn't burning. Add the honey, lemon juice, and cinnamon. Remove the cover and continue cooking over low heat for another 15 minutes. The texture should be thick and jammy, and the mixture will look glossy. Add the walnuts and stir to incorporate. Continue to cook, uncovered, for another 15 minutes. Stir frequently to avoid burning.

For the coconut coating

¼ cup (20 grams) unsweet-
ened shredded coconut
(optional)

1 teaspoon grated orange
zest (optional)

4. **Cool the mixture:** Spoon the mixture onto a piece of parchment paper or a silicone mat and let cool for 1 hour.

5. **Shape and coat:** In a small bowl, combine the coconut and orange zest (if using). Spread the matzo meal and coconut mixtures on 2 separate medium plates. Divide the prune mixture into 4 equal-size pieces and roll each piece into a log about 9 inches long and 1½ inches in diameter. The log will be sticky. Roll the log in either the matzo meal or coconut mixture. The coating will help you smooth out the shape of the logs. Repeat with the remaining prune mixture.

6. **Store:** Wrap the logs in plastic wrap. Refrigerate for about 1 hour to firm them up. (They do not need to stay refrigerated.) Slice on the diagonal and serve as a snack or dessert.

Berry Fruit Compote

PREP TIME: 5 minutes • **COOK TIME:** 15 minutes

When my kids were younger, I made pancakes every Sunday morning. One weekend, I was nearly out of syrup but had plenty of fruit, so I whipped up a fruit compote—and thus this recipe was born. This technique works with fresh or frozen fruit, so think beyond pancakes and enjoy with New York–Style Cheesecake Bars (page 98), Blintz Casserole (page 62), Citrus Sponge Cake (page 102), ice cream, yogurt, and so much more. ✳ MAKES 1 CUP

2 cups (394 grams) frozen or fresh mixed berries

2 tablespoons granulated sugar, honey, maple syrup, or agave nectar

½ teaspoon grated lemon zest or orange zest

1 tablespoon freshly squeezed lemon juice or orange juice

1 teaspoon vanilla

1. **Boil:** In a medium saucepan, combine the berries, sugar, zest, juice, and vanilla. Cook over medium heat until boiling, about 5 minutes.

2. **Simmer:** Turn the heat to medium-low and simmer for about 10 more minutes. The berries will begin to break down, but some large chunks will remain. For a smoother compote, use a masher or wooden spoon to crush the chunks of fruit. Remove from the heat and let cool—as it cools, it will continue to thicken.

Bubbe's Matzo Meal Pancake

PREP TIME: 10 minutes • **COOK TIME:** 5 minutes

I have such happy memories of the flavors of this simple, unfussy dish that I insisted my mother teach me how to make it. When I posted the recipe on my blog a while back, I received this heartwarming note from my cousin: *"For the duration of the meal tonight, I was 10 years old again and back at Avenue N with my mommy and Grandma in the kitchen. It was a truly wonderful and sentimental moment for me."* I hope this super-simple, single-serving recipe brings you as much comfort as it has brought me. ✳ SERVES 1 TO 2

For the pancake

2 large eggs, separated

2 tablespoons matzo meal

1 tablespoon seltzer water

¼ teaspoon kosher salt

1 tablespoon vegetable oil

For the topping

1 teaspoon granulated sugar

¼ teaspoon cinnamon

Sweet wine (optional)

1. **Mix:** In a medium bowl, whisk together the egg yolks, matzo meal, seltzer, and salt. Set aside.

2. **Whip:** In another medium bowl, whip the egg whites until they form stiff peaks.

3. **Fold batter:** Carefully fold the egg-white mixture into the yolk mixture.

4. **Panfry:** Heat the oil in an 8-inch skillet set over medium to medium-high heat. When the oil starts to shimmer, add the matzo meal mixture and continue cooking it until you see it sizzle around the edges and begin to firm up, about a minute. Using a spatula, flip the pancake and let it cook for about 30 more seconds, until golden brown on both sides.

5. **Serve:** Serve the pancake sprinkled with the sugar and cinnamon. To get the same effect as my cousin did, enjoy a little sweet wine on top as well.

Dana's Ultimate Sweet Apple Noodle Kugel

PREP TIME: 25 minutes • **COOK TIME:** 1 hour 5 minutes

On her *Foodie Goes Healthy* blog, my friend Dana describes feeling the presence of her family members in the kitchen when she's cooking traditional foods. She imagines the comments her father might make and remembers her mother's prowess at hosting a great party. This kugel manifests those warm memories, and cleverly wraps components from all of Dana's favorite sweet kugels into one wonderful recipe. ✳ SERVES 16

1 (12-ounce) package wide egg noodles

Vegetable oil, for boiling the noodles

8 ounces (232 grams) cream cheese, softened

1¾ cups (427 grams) milk, whole or low-fat, warmed (100°F to 115°F)

6 tablespoons (85 grams) unsalted butter, melted, plus more for greasing

1 cup (226 grams) small-curd cottage cheese, regular or low-fat

¾ cup (141 grams) granulated sugar

2 teaspoons vanilla extract

2 teaspoons cinnamon, divided

1 teaspoon kosher salt

6 large eggs, beaten

2 Granny Smith apples, peeled, cored, and diced small

1. **Preheat/Prep:** Preheat the oven to 350°F and adjust the oven rack to the center shelf. Grease a 9-by-13-inch glass baking dish with butter.

2. **Boil:** Bring a large pot of salted water to a boil, and add a few drops of oil to prevent the noodles from sticking together. Boil the egg noodles for 5 minutes, until softened but still a little firm. Drain and set aside.

3. **Mix:** In a very large bowl using an electric hand mixer, beat together the cream cheese, milk, and butter. Mix in the cottage cheese, sugar, vanilla, 1 teaspoon of cinnamon, the salt, and the beaten eggs and stir until well combined. Gently fold in the noodles and diced apples until evenly incorporated.

4. **Pour:** Pour the mixture into the baking pan and sprinkle the remaining 1 teaspoon of cinnamon on top.

5. **Bake:** Bake the kugel for 1 hour, checking at 40 minutes to see if the top is browning. If it looks like the top might burn, tent the kugel with foil and continue baking for the remaining 20 minutes. Bake until the center is set and the top of the kugel is golden brown. Cool at least 10 minutes; then cut into squares to serve.

Make-ahead Tip: Assemble the kugel through step 4 and refrigerate overnight. The next day, leave the kugel out at room temperature for 30 minutes before baking as usual.

Variation Tip: Make a crunchy topping by combining 2 cups of crushed cornflakes or 1 cup of chopped nuts with ¼ cup of brown sugar and 4 tablespoons of melted butter. Sprinkle on top before baking.

Savory Matzo Farfel Kugel

PREP TIME: 20 minutes • **COOK TIME:** 35 minutes

When I first posted a recipe for a sweet matzo farfel kugel on my blog, it went viral. This savory farfel version is my most recent addition. Adding herbs, vegetables, and whipped egg whites lightens it up, and a quick pass under the broiler yields a satisfying, crispy finish for this Passover kugel. ✳ SERVES 8

4 sheets matzah

1½ cups (360 grams) chicken, vegetable, or beef stock or water

1 medium onion, diced

1 to 2 tablespoons olive oil, plus more for greasing baking dish

1 tablespoon dried thyme

3 large eggs, separated

1 teaspoon kosher salt

1 teaspoon black pepper

¼ cup (15 grams) chopped fresh parsley

1 medium carrot, shredded (about ½ cup/21 grams)

1. **Preheat/Prep:** Preheat the oven to 350°F. Grease an 8-by-8-inch baking dish with olive oil. Place the matzo sheets in a plastic bag or on a cutting board underneath a towel and use a rolling pin to crush them into farfel-size pieces. In a medium bowl, pour the stock over the farfel and set aside.

2. **Sauté:** In a medium skillet over medium heat, sauté the onion, olive oil, and thyme until the onion is translucent and beginning to brown, about 7 to 10 minutes. Set aside to cool.

3. **Whip:** In a small bowl, lightly whisk the egg yolks. In a medium bowl, whip the egg whites until they form firm peaks.

4. **Mix:** To the soaked farfel, add the salt, pepper, egg yolks, chopped parsley, shredded carrot, and sautéed onion. Stir to combine.

5. **Fold mixture:** Using a spatula, gently fold the egg whites into the farfel mixture until combined.

6. **Bake:** Pour the mixture into the prepared baking dish. Bake for about 30 minutes until it is golden brown. Set the oven to broil and broil until crispy on top, about 3 minutes.

Variation Tip: If you like a crispy-bottomed crust, preheat the baking dish with 2 teaspoons of olive oil before you pour in the farfel mixture. Be careful to avoid splattering; return the pan to the oven immediately.

Challah Bread Pudding

PREP TIME: 15 minutes • **INACTIVE TIME:** 10 minutes • **COOK TIME:** 30 minutes

This French toast–style bread pudding is the number one best way to use up leftover challah, not to mention spare fruit. My recipe calls for fresh peaches and blueberries, but I encourage you to use what you have on hand and adjust the fruit to match the season. (Even dried fruit would be a nice addition.) Don't be afraid to substitute here. You can replace the milk with a dairy-free milk alternative, half-and-half, or heavy whipping cream. ✶ SERVES 4 TO 6

Butter, for greasing
  the dish

3 large eggs

1⅓ cups milk (340 grams),
  whole or low-fat

¼ cup (62 grams) freshly
  squeezed orange juice

¼ cup (60 grams)
  maple syrup

½ teaspoon vanilla extract

Zest of ½ lemon

½ teaspoon cinnamon

½ teaspoon salt

Half a 1-pound loaf
  Bubbe's Challah
  (page 22), cut into
  1-inch cubes

1 cup (140 grams) fresh
  blueberries, divided

1 medium peach,
  skin on, seeded and
  chopped, divided

Berry Fruit Compote
  (page 110), for serving
  (optional)

Maple syrup, for serving
  (optional)

1. **Preheat/Prep:** Preheat the oven to 375°F. Grease an 8-by-8-inch baking dish with butter.

2. **Mix:** In a medium bowl, whisk together the eggs, milk, orange juice, maple syrup, vanilla, lemon zest, cinnamon, and salt. Add the bread cubes and ¾ of the blueberries and peach and mix with a large spoon.

3. **Pour:** Pour the egg and bread mixture into the baking dish. Let sit for 10 minutes to allow the bread to soak up the liquid. Scatter the rest of the blueberries and peach on top.

4. **Bake:** Bake the bread pudding for 25 to 30 minutes. It will puff up, and once it's ready, a toothpick inserted in the center will come out clean. Cool on a wire rack or protected surface for about 10 minutes. Serve warm, with Berry Fruit Compote or maple syrup (if using).

Make-ahead Tip: After step 3, cover and refrigerate the pudding overnight. Bake the following morning, allowing for 5 extra minutes of baking time because it will be chilled.

DAIRY-FREE, GLUTEN-FREE, PAREVE

Sandi's Honey Sesame Candy

PREP TIME: 20 minutes • **INACTIVE TIME:** 15 minutes • **COOK TIME:** 10 minutes

Sesame seeds are probably best known as a popular topper for bagels or the source of tahini, but they're also the base of a delicious candy. Made with honey, this treat is an ideal addition to any Rosh Hashanah dessert tray or holiday gift basket. My friend Sandi Gaertner, of the gluten-free blog *Fearless Dining*, gave me her recipe to share with you. ✱ MAKES 64 PIECES

2 cups (256 grams) raw sesame seeds
½ cup (170 grams) honey
½ cup (110 grams) brown sugar
½ teaspoon cinnamon
½ teaspoon ground ginger
½ teaspoon kosher salt
Nonstick cooking spray

1. **Prep:** Line a baking sheet with a silicone mat or parchment paper. (If using parchment, tape it down to the baking sheet so it won't move around when you spread the candy mixture.)

2. **Toast the seeds:** In a medium skillet, toast the sesame seeds over medium heat for 3 to 5 minutes until they start turning brown and release their nutty aroma. Watch carefully—they'll burn easily.

3. **Boil the candy mixture:** In a medium pot, combine the honey, brown sugar, cinnamon, ginger, and salt and bring to a boil, stirring constantly. Once the mixture reaches a rolling boil, stop stirring and cook for 2 minutes. Remove the pot from the heat and stir in the sesame seeds, mixing well.

4. **Form the candy:** Pour the mixture onto the prepared baking sheet. Working quickly and using a metal spoon, spatula, or offset spatula dipped in cold water or sprayed with nonstick spray, press the candy into a flat, even layer, about ¼ inch thick.

5. **Cool:** Allow the candy to cool for 15 minutes, or until lukewarm to the touch. Transfer the cooled candy to a large cutting board. Prepare a sheet of wax paper or parchment paper.

6. **Cut:** Using a sharp knife, cut the candy into roughly 2-by-1-inch pieces, working quickly before it hardens too much. Lay the pieces of candy on the wax or parchment paper.

7. **Wrap (optional):** Cut the paper around each candy, allowing room for folding (roughly 4-by-4-inch squares work well). Fold the wax paper or parchment over each piece of candy and twist the edges to close.

8. **Store:** If not wrapping the candy, store the pieces layered between parchment or wax paper in an airtight container for up to 2 weeks.

Variation Tip: Mix white sesame seeds with black sesame seeds for a more dramatic-looking candy.

Bimuelos with Orange Syrup

PREP TIME: 15 minutes • **INACTIVE TIME:** 1 hour • **COOK TIME:** 15 minutes for the syrup, plus 6 minutes per fritter

Bimuelos are a Sephardic Hanukkah specialty, closer to a free-form fritter than a donut. Bimuelos dough is loose, like a batter, and is spooned directly into hot oil, rather than formed and then fried. ✳ MAKES 12 TO 15 FRITTERS

For the dough

3 cups (375 grams)
   all-purpose flour

2¼ teaspoons
   (7g/1 packet) active dry
   or instant yeast

1 tablespoon
   granulated sugar

½ teaspoon kosher salt

1 teaspoon cinnamon

1 teaspoon grated
   orange zest

1½ cups (353 grams) warm
   water (105°F to 115°F)

1 tablespoon vegetable oil

½ cup (124 grams) freshly
   squeezed orange juice

Vegetable oil, for frying

For the syrup
and topping

½ cup (170 grams) honey

¼ cup (47 grams)
   granulated sugar

¼ cup (59 grams) water

3 strips orange rind

¼ cup powdered sugar

1 teaspoon flake salt

1. **Mix the dough:** In a medium bowl, whisk together the flour, yeast, granulated sugar, salt, cinnamon, and orange zest. Add the water, oil, and orange juice and mix with a wooden spoon, until no dry spots remain.

2. **Rise:** Cover the bowl with a towel. Set aside to rise until bubbly and doubled in size, about 1 hour.

3. **Boil the syrup:** In a small saucepan, boil the honey, granulated sugar, water, and orange rind. Reduce the heat to low and simmer for 10 to 15 minutes, until the syrup is thick but still pourable. Remove the syrup from the heat and set aside to cool.

4. **Prepare for frying:** Line a platter with paper towels. Heat 3 to 4 inches of oil in a medium saucepan to 350°F.

5. **Deep-fry:** Using a large spoon or a cookie scoop, drop heaping tablespoons of the dough into the oil, avoiding overcrowding. Fry for 2 to 3 minutes on each side, depending on the size of the fritter. Once browned on one side, flip with a spoon and brown the other side. Remove the with a slotted spoon to the prepared platter. Repeat with the rest of the batter. Serve immediately, sprinkled with the powdered sugar and salt (if using) and with the syrup drizzled on top or served on the side.

Baked or Fried Soufganiyot (Jelly Donuts)

PREP TIME: 40 minutes • **INACTIVE TIME:** 1 hour 30 minutes • **COOK TIME:** 10 minutes

Who doesn't love a donut, especially when you can justify it as a way to celebrate the miracle of oil for Hanukkah? This versatile dough works well either baked or fried—just follow the instructions for either method of cooking. You'll end up with a delicious result no matter what. Feel free to get creative with the flavor of the jam filling, but be sure to use a jam thin enough to flow through the decorating tip. ✱ MAKES 14 TO 16 DONUTS

For the dough

2¼ cups (281 grams) all-purpose flour, plus more for dusting and kneading

3 tablespoons granulated sugar

2¼ teaspoons (7 grams/1 packet) active dry or instant yeast

½ teaspoon kosher salt

⅔ cup (161 grams) warm milk (105°F to 115°F)

2 tablespoons (27 grams) vegetable oil, plus more to oil the bowl

1 large egg

½ teaspoon vanilla extract

1 teaspoon grated lemon zest or orange zest (optional)

1. **Mix:** In a medium bowl, whisk together the flour, sugar, yeast, and salt. Add the milk, oil, egg, vanilla, and lemon zest (if using), and mix with a wooden spoon until a rough, wet dough forms.

2. **Knead:** Place the dough on a well-floured surface, dust the top of the dough with flour, and knead for about 2 minutes. If it remains sticky while kneading, add more flour 1 tablespoon at a time. It should be tacky but not too sticky to knead.

3. **Rise:** Oil the bowl you just used and place the dough back inside. Cover with a towel and let it rise until doubled in size, about 1 hour.

4. **Roll the dough:** Line a baking sheet with parchment paper. On a floured surface, roll out the dough to ½ inch thick.

5. **Cut the donuts:** Using a 2½-inch round cookie cutter or the rim of a glass, cut out as many rounds as you can and place them on the prepared baking sheet. Re-roll the remaining scraps and repeat. You should have 14 to 16 rounds total.

CONTINUED ▸

For baking/frying and coating

2 tablespoons unsalted butter, melted (if baking)

Vegetable oil (if frying)

1 cup granulated sugar

For the filling

¾ cup (240 grams) seedless jam

6. **Second rise:** Cover the baking sheet with a kitchen towel and let the donuts rise until they puff up slightly, about 30 minutes, depending on the temperature of the kitchen.

To bake the donuts (Method 1)

1. **Prep for baking:** While the donuts rise, preheat the oven to 375°F.

2. **Bake:** After the donuts have risen, bake them for about 10 minutes, until golden. While the donuts bake, melt the butter. When the donuts come out of the oven, brush each of the donuts with the melted butter. Proceed immediately to Finish the donuts (page 121).

To deep-fry the donuts (Method 2)

1. **Prep for frying:** Add vegetable oil to a medium pot, at least 2 inches deep. Heat the oil to 350°F. Line a baking sheet with paper towels to drain any excess oil.

2. **Deep-fry:** Place a few donuts at a time in the hot oil, avoiding overcrowding. Fry for 1 minute on one side; then flip and fry on the second side for 1 minute, until golden brown. This is a fast process, so watch carefully. Once fried, transfer the donuts to the prepared baking sheet. Proceed immediately to Finish the donuts (page 121).

Filling the soufganiyot

To finish the donuts

1. **Coat the donuts:** Place the sugar in a gallon-size resealable plastic bag. Working one at a time, place each donut in the bag of sugar, seal shut, and shake it around to coat the donut. Return the donut to the baking sheet. Repeat with all donuts.

2. **Fill donuts:** Fit a piping bag (or a plastic bag) with a decorating tip with a ¼-inch-wide opening. Fill the bag with the jam of your choice. Using a paring knife, cut a 1-inch horizontal slit in the side of each donut, slicing through to the center. Place the decorating tip in the hole and squeeze until the jam starts to ooze out of the donut (some spillage is okay). Repeat with the remaining donuts. The donuts taste best if served immediately, but they will maintain their freshness for several hours.

Taiglach with Honey Ginger Syrup

PREP TIME: 30 minutes • **INACTIVE TIME:** 5 minutes • **COOK TIME:** 1 hour

Making taiglach, a Rosh Hashanah treat, is like taking a journey back in time. Rarely seen in bakeries today, the simple dough balls are cooked in a fragrant honey syrup (sometimes baked or fried first). For a dramatic, festive presentation, these sticky spheres can be assembled together in the shape of Mount Sinai—somewhat like a French croquembouche in appearance, though not flavor. Nuts and dried fruits, especially maraschino cherries, are often added as a traditional topping.

MAKES 12 TAIGLACH

For the dough

3 large eggs plus 1 egg yolk

3 tablespoons
   vegetable oil

1 teaspoon vanilla extract

1¾ cups (219 grams)
   all-purpose flour, plus
   more for kneading

1 teaspoon baking powder

½ teaspoon kosher salt

2 teaspoons ground ginger

For the syrup

1 cup (340 grams) honey

1 cup (188 grams)
   granulated sugar

1 cup (235 grams) water

1-inch knob of fresh
   ginger, peeled and sliced

1 cinnamon stick
   (optional)

2 tablespoons freshly
   squeezed lemon juice

1 teaspoon grated
   lemon zest

1 cup (160 grams) mixed
   nuts and/or dried fruits

1. **Preheat/Prep:** Preheat the oven to 375°F. Line 2 baking sheets with parchment paper.

2. **Mix the dough:** In a medium bowl, whisk together the eggs, egg yolk, oil, and vanilla. Sift together the flour, baking powder, salt, and ginger into the egg mixture. Stir until a shaggy dough forms. In the bowl, knead the dough for a minute or two. The dough should be soft and smooth but not sticky. If it's too wet, add flour, 1 tablespoon at a time up to 4 tablespoons, until the dough is easy to handle. Cover with a kitchen towel or plastic wrap and let it rest for 10 minutes.

3. **Form the taiglach:** Take about a quarter of the dough and, using both hands, roll it out into a long thin rope, about ½ inch in diameter. If the dough is a touch sticky, lightly flour your hands and it will easily roll out. With a small knife, cut ½-inch pieces and place them cut side down, 1-inch apart, on the prepared baking sheet.

4. **Bake:** Half the dough will fill one baking sheet. Bake the first set for 7 minutes. While they bake, prepare the other half of the dough. Remove the baked taiglach to a wire cooling rack and use the baking sheet to bake the second batch for 7 minutes.

5. **Boil the syrup:** Once the second sheet is in the oven, prepare the syrup. In a medium saucepan, heat the honey, sugar, water, ginger, cinnamon stick (if using), lemon juice, and lemon zest until the sugar dissolves and the mixture is boiling. Turn the heat down to low, cover the pot, and continue to simmer for 5 to 7 minutes.

6. **Simmer:** Drop the baked balls into the simmering syrup. Stir the foamy mixture and cover the pot, keeping the temperature as low as possible. As it cooks, the syrup and the dough balls will darken. Simmer the balls for about 35 minutes, stirring every 15 minutes. Do not turn the heat up to try to rush the process, because the syrup will harden like candy and become unusable. After 35 minutes, add the nuts and/or dried fruits and continue to cook uncovered for 10 more minutes, bringing the mixture back to a low boil. If you have an instant-read thermometer, the temperature of the syrup should be around 230°F, which is equivalent to the soft-ball stage of candy. The syrup and balls should also appear much darker than they did at the start of the cooking.

7. **Cool:** Place 12 cupcake liners on a baking sheet. After the balls and nuts finish cooking in the syrup, remove the cinnamon stick and sliced ginger pieces. Spoon the mixture into the liners. Cool completely before serving. The taiglach will keep for up to 2 weeks in an airtight container.

Measurement Conversions

VOLUME EQUIVALENTS	US STANDARD	US STANDARD (OUNCES)	METRIC (APPROXIMATE)
LIQUID	2 tablespoons	1 fl. oz.	30 mL
	¼ cup	2 fl. oz.	60 mL
	½ cup	4 fl. oz.	120 mL
	1 cup	8 fl. oz.	240 mL
	1½ cups	12 fl. oz.	355 mL
	2 cups or 1 pint	16 fl. oz.	475 mL
	4 cups or 1 quart	32 fl. oz.	1 L
	1 gallon	128 fl. oz.	4 L
DRY	⅛ teaspoon	–	0.5 mL
	¼ teaspoon	–	1 mL
	½ teaspoon	–	2 mL
	¾ teaspoon	–	4 mL
	1 teaspoon	–	5 mL
	1 tablespoon	–	15 mL
	¼ cup	–	59 mL
	⅓ cup	–	79 mL
	½ cup	–	118 mL
	⅔ cup	–	156 mL
	¾ cup	–	177 mL
	1 cup	–	235 mL
	2 cups or 1 pint	–	475 mL
	3 cups	–	700 mL
	4 cups or 1 quart	–	1 L
	½ gallon	–	2 L
	1 gallon	–	4 L

OVEN TEMPERATURES

FAHRENHEIT	CELSIUS (APPROXIMATE)
250°F	120°C
300°F	150°C
325°F	165°C
350°F	180°C
375°F	190°C
400°F	200°C
425°F	220°C
450°F	230°C

WEIGHT EQUIVALENTS

US STANDARD	METRIC (APPROXIMATE)
½ ounce	15 g
1 ounce	30 g
2 ounces	60 g
4 ounces	115 g
8 ounces	225 g
12 ounces	340 g
16 ounces or 1 pound	455 g

Resources

My research for this book spanned friends, family, rabbis, colleagues, cookbooks, and a myriad of online resources. Below is a selection, by no means complete, of some of the resources I used along the way.

Books

Edlin, Rosabelle, and Shushannah Spector. *Adventures in Jewish Cooking*. New York: Galahad Books, 1964.

Goldstein, Joyce. *The New Mediterranean Jewish Table*. Oakland: University of California Press, 2016.

Kander, Lizzie Black (compiled). *The Settlement Cookbook*. Milwaukee: The Settlement Cookbook Company, 1941.

Marks, Gil. *The World of Jewish Desserts*. New York: Simon & Schuster, 2000.

Menashe, Solomon. *Our Sephardic Delicacies from Rhodes*. Phoenix: Menashe Consulting, 2008.

Nathan, Joan. *The Foods of Israel Today*. New York: Knopf, 2010.

Nathan, Joan. *Jewish Holiday Cookbook*. New York: Schocken Books, 2004.

Nathan, Joan. *King Solomon's Table*. New York: Alfred A. Knopf, 2017.

Ottolenghi, Yotam, and Sami Tamimi. *Jerusalem: A Cookbook*. Berkeley: Ten Speed Press, 2012.

Roden, Claudia. *The Book of Jewish Food*. New York: Alfred A. Knopf, 1996

Roseman, Pearl, ed. *Cooking the Sephardic Way: Presented by the Sephardic Sisterhood Temple Tifereth Israel*. California: North American Press, 1971.

Sokolov, Raymond. *The Jewish-American Kitchen*. New York: Stewart, Tabori & Chang, 1989.

Sussman, Adeena. *Sababa*. New York: Avery, 2019.

Tamimi, Sami, and Tara Wigley. *Falastin: A Cookbook*. Berkeley: Ten Speed Press, 2020.

Online Resources

Aqua-Calc: Aqua-Calc.com/calculate/food-volume-to-weight

Bendichas Manos (blog): BendichasManos.com

Bob's Red Mill Natural Foods: BobsRedMill.com

Cinnamon Shtick (blog): CinnamonShtick.com

Fine Cooking magazine: FineCooking.com

Fleischmann's Yeast: FleischmannsYeast.com

Food & Wine magazine: FoodandWine.com

Food52: Food52.com

The Forward: Forward.com

Jamie Geller (blog): JamieGeller.com

Jewish Food Experience: JewishFoodExperience.com

King Arthur Baking: KingArthurBaking.com

The Little Ferraro Kitchen (blog): LittleFerraroKitchen.com

Los Angeles Times: LATimes.com

Jewish Cooking (Facebook group): Facebook.com/groups/174618965938157

Jewish Holiday Cooking (Facebook group): Facebook.com/groups
/jewishholidaycooking/

My Jewish Learning: MyJewishLearning.com

My Name Is Yeh (blog): MyNameisYeh.com

New York Times: NYTimes.com

Once Upon a Chef (blog): OnceUponaChef.com

Red Star Yeast: RedStarYeast.com

NPR's *The Salt* (blog): NPR.org/sections/thesalt

Sephardic Spice SEC FOOD (Facebook group): Facebook.com /groups/184382281991699

Serious Eats: SeriousEats.com

Tablet magazine: TabletMag.com

What Jew Wanna Eat (Facebook group): Facebook.com/whatjewwannaeat

Index

ACKNOWLEDGMENTS

Writing a cookbook is a challenging and exhilarating process. Doing so during a pandemic is a bit like running a marathon. I could not have completed this project without a tireless team of testers, tasters, and texters. Many of my text message conversations were so integral to my success that I would add them to my bibliography if it were possible.

To my quarantined husband and daughter, who temporarily lost their household savory cook but gained an endless supply of baked goods: Thank you for encouraging me and for eating *dessert first* over and over again. To my angel Gregory, who sits on my shoulder always and would be so glad I wrote this book.

To Callisto Media: Thank you to the talented editorial and production team for helping me to create a cookbook for the world to enjoy. (My bubbe would be kvelling.)

ABOUT THE AUTHOR

 **BETH A. LEE** grew up on the East Coast before moving with her family to Northern California, thousands of miles away from the traditional Jewish food she was raised on. She attended the University of California, Berkeley, where she received a degree in business and later pursued a marketing career in Silicon Valley. In 2010, Beth realized she preferred pita chips over computer chips and launched her food blog, *OMG! Yummy*. Through her blog, she reconnected with her love of cooking and her passion for documenting her family's multicultural food traditions. Beth has been featured in the *New York Times* and the *San Jose Mercury News* and has been a frequent contributor to *Edible Silicon Valley*. She also co-leads a popular virtual cooking group, *Tasting Jerusalem*, focused on Middle Eastern cuisines and ingredients. Beth is so glad she can make a New York–style bagel in her sunlit kitchen in Northern California.

CPSIA information can be obtained
at www.ICGtesting.com
Printed in the USA
LVHW071009220821
695824LV00002B/2